The Certainties in Trading

31 Hard Truths About Markets — None About How to Win

John Xu

THE CERTAINTIES IN TRADING

31 Hard Truths About Markets — None About How to Win

Translated from the Chinese 《交易中确定的事》. Portions of this book were produced with the assistance of artificial intelligence, including the English translation.

ISBN 978-1-7648987-0-6 (paperback)
ISBN 978-1-7648987-1-3 (ebook)

First edition, 2026

Published by XWise Press

Contents

Preface

This book is the product of a long argument between a trader and a machine: the propositions were put by the human, hammered by the AI, and adjudicated by the human—nothing was admitted until both sides had gone over it without mercy. The author has collected these certainties of trading into a single volume, offered to fellow traders for reference and for argument.

Part One

The Certainty of Rules and Costs

Chapter One

The Accident Written on the Timetable

Certainty 1: The rules of the trading session are certain. Gaps and vacuums are not accidents. They happen only at certain hours.

January 3, 2019, a few minutes past 7:30 in the morning, Tokyo time.

Anyone who trades currencies knows how empty that hour is. New York has closed. London is asleep. Sydney has never had the liquidity to hold a room. And Tokyo, the only desk due to take over—Tokyo was shut for the Japanese New Year holiday. At that moment the global foreign exchange market was about as thin as it gets in any given year: the machines were still quoting, but there was almost nobody behind the order book.

Inside a few minutes, USD/JPY fell from around 108.6 straight through to 104.9—four hundred pips in seven minutes, one of the largest single-day moves in a decade. Against the Australian dollar the yen ran almost 8 percent; against the Turkish lira, close to 10. Within the hour most of it had come back, as though nothing had happened at all.

The post-mortems turned up plenty of "reasons." The night before, Apple had cut its revenue guidance—a rare event—and lit a fuse under risk sentiment. Japanese retail traders were sitting on piles of Australian dollars and Turkish lira, carry trades funded in yen; as the yen firmed, their stops went off in layers, each stop becoming fresh selling, each wave of selling reaching down to detonate the stops beneath it. Trend-following algorithms smelled blood and joined the chase, and the stampede was amplified one more time. Japan's STP brokers absorbed several million dollars of negative-balance losses that day—money their clients had lost and could not repay, so the brokers ate it.

All of that is second-order. The first-order reason is a good deal plainer: **the same selling, dropped into the order book during the London–New York overlap, might not have produced a single candle worth looking at.** The killer that morning was not Apple, not the retail crowd, not the algorithms. It was the timetable. The stampede happened inside the one window where market structure is weakest, and the location of that window is printed on a trading calendar anyone can look up: every day, between the New York close and the Tokyo open, doubled on every Japanese holiday, doubled again in the first days of a year when liquidity has not yet come back to its desk.

The triple vacuum of that morning—the daily one, the holiday one, the turn-of-the-year one—was not a black swan. **A black swan cannot be foreseen. That window keeps a class schedule.** The only unforeseeable part is which day a spark happens to fall into it.

* * *

THAT IS THE WHOLE OF THE FIRST CERTAINTY, AND SAID PLAINLY IT is disappointingly simple: **when there are people in the market and when there are not is fixed by the rules.**

Exchange-traded instruments are the blunt case: the open and the close are written into the rulebook. Foreign exchange advertises itself as a twenty-four-hour market, a show that never closes, but its version of the certainty is hiding somewhere else—**between the New York close on Friday and the Sydney open on Sunday, there is no price for your instrument anywhere on this planet.** For more than forty hours the world goes on as usual: central bankers give speeches, wars break out, companies blow up—there is simply no price putting a number on any of it. The instant quoting resumes on Sunday, a weekend of accumulated information is released in a single print. That is a gap.

The most underrated thing about a gap is this: **it voids your stop.** In the hours with no quotes your stop order is waste paper—the price does not travel through your level, it appears on the other side of it. A stop you set a few pips from Friday's close can fill hundreds of pips beyond it on Sunday, and that distance in between, the distance you believed you were protected across, was never protected at all. (The stop order itself has a finer account to settle, and that is the next chapter's business.)

The intraday vacuum of January 3 is the same thing in miniature: the quotes are still there, but the depth is gone. An order book that is inches thick on an ordinary afternoon is paper-thin for those few hours, and an order that would normally mean nothing is now the one that takes out the last bid. The sterling flash crash of October 2016 also happened around seven in the morning in Asia; nearly every famous currency flash crash since has fallen inside the same handful of windows. **The accidents cluster so tightly that calling them accidents begins to feel dishonest.**

* * *

Push this certainty downward and you get three corollaries.

First, to hold a position through a vacuum is to hold unpriced risk. Carrying a position over the weekend is selling an option and collecting no premium for it: whatever happens between Friday and Sunday, you can neither respond to it nor step out of the way. This does not mean you may never hold over a weekend—trend systems often must—but it does mean the decision deserves to be made as a risk decision in its own right, rather than by the inertia of just leaving it on. Position size, stop distance, whether to cut in half on Friday: all of it should be priced with the gap in view.

Second, pin the accident calendar to your system. Japanese holidays, American holidays, the turn of the year, the daily vacuum hours—these dates and times are public, free, and available years in advance. A system that does not so much as glance at the trading calendar is marching blindfolded across a mapped minefield. Do one single thing, open no new position during the liquidity vacuum, and you have already stayed off the scene of most of the flash crashes in the history of the currency market.

Third, and this one runs through the whole book: find the rules first, look at the market second. The Japanese retail traders who blew through their accounts that morning did not lose to bad judgment—on the question of whether the yen should rise, with hindsight, they had not even got the frame wrong. They lost because they never put the fact that Tokyo is closed today into the risk decision. The market is uncertain; the calendar is certain. **To lose to uncertainty is bad luck. To lose to certainty is homework you did not do.**

The same hour, the same accident—that is not coincidence, it is a certainty, and certainties are what this book is about. They have nothing to do with the reading of price and volume; that is technique, and reasonable people differ. These are facts of market structure that exist prior to any price action—independent of judgment, identical for everyone, already in the room before the accident begins. The market takes most people's money by way of uncertainty, but uncertainty never detonates out of thin air. It blows along a seam of certainty: at a certain hour of vacuum, at a certain stop level, on certain leverage arithmetic. What follows is an attempt to dig those seams out one at a time and set them in order.

(*End of Chapter One*)

CHAPTER TWO

Two Promises, One Kept

Certainty 2: A stop order's trigger is certain. Its fill price is not.

JANUARY 15, 2015, HALF PAST TEN IN THE MORNING, ZURICH TIME.

The Swiss National Bank published a statement a few lines long: effective immediately, it was abandoning the 1.20 floor under EUR/CHF.

To feel the weight of those few lines you have to know what the floor was. From September 2011 the SNB had publicly committed to buying euros at whatever cost was required to hold the rate above 1.20—and for more than three years it did exactly what it said, so the market came to believe it. Below 1.20 was not a support level. It was a sovereign's word. Days before the collapse the bank's vice chairman was still calling the floor "a pillar of our monetary policy." Traders around the world leaned on that pillar, went long EUR/CHF, and tucked their stops just beneath 1.20. The logic was airtight: how far can a floor fall with a central bank standing on it?

At half past ten the pillar was pulled away. To call what followed a crash is inaccurate—a crash at least involves the process of falling, and what happened that morning was that **the price simply vanished.** Within seconds of the announcement EUR/CHF was through 1.20. Within two minutes, executable liquidity on the major platforms was approaching zero. For the next forty minutes or so, in one of the most liquid currency pairs on earth, almost nobody was quoting: bids on the big ECNs differed from one another by thousands of pips, and a few platforms printed ghost prices of 0.5 and below. When the dust settled the rate stood near 1.04. And at the low—a G10 currency pair, in one morning, down almost 30 percent.

Now for the people who were "protected."

A London retail client named Novak was long EUR/CHF at IG on roughly £600 of notional. He had done everything the textbook asks. He had a stop, fifty pips below the 1.20 floor—by the market consensus of the previous three years, an extremely conservative placement. His stop did trigger, on time, to the second. It filled near 0.92. **More than two thousand seven hundred pips from where he had put it.** When the account was settled he had not merely lost his stake; he owed the broker £21,171. A £600 position, a debt of more than twenty thousand pounds. This is not an urban legend. It is on the record in the trade press, and it went before the British financial ombudsman.

He was not unusual. That day, account after account went straight from profit to a negative balance. Alpari, an established British broker, declared itself insolvent before the session was out. FXCM, listed in New York, booked $225 million of client negative balances and survived only on an emergency rescue. The second-by-second data FXCM published afterward showed that by the **ninth second** after the break of 1.20, the volume it could still match had fallen to a rounding error—most of the stop orders were standing in a queue, and at the head of the queue there was no longer a market.

* * *

THE CERTAINTY OF THIS CHAPTER IS INSIDE NOVAK'S SINGLE TRADE, and it takes one sentence: **a stop order is two promises, and the market keeps only the first.**

The first promise: when the price touches the level you set, the order is activated. That one is iron. It is written into the code of the trading system, and it held perfectly that morning—every stop fired exactly on time.

The second promise—that you will be filled somewhere near the price you set—**never existed.** It is a default assumption living in almost everybody's head. The moment a stop is triggered it becomes a market order: price no object, take the first counterparty in the queue it can reach. (This is the default on nearly every retail platform—a stop market. There is another kind, a stop limit, which converts to a limit order on trigger; it protects your price at the cost of possibly not filling at all. Two promises, and you may choose exactly one to have kept.) On ordinary days the other side is packed in behind you within a few pips, and so the illusion that the trigger price is the fill price gets confirmed again and again, day after day—until the day there is nobody behind you at all, and your market order goes hunting downward for someone willing to take the other side. Wherever it finds one, that is your fill. Novak's twenty-seven-hundred-pip slippage was not a system failure. **It was a stop order faithfully executing, in empty country, the only instruction it ever really carries: get out now, whatever it costs.**

The last chapter dealt with gaps: in the hours with no quotes, the price appears on the far side of your stop. The franc demonstrates the other way to die: the quotes never stopped, but there was no size behind them. Two roads, one destination—**your stop level marks where you want to get out, not where you can.**

Someone will ask about the guaranteed stop. It exists: some brokers sell one—they promise a fill at your price and swallow the slippage themselves. Note the word sell. The wider spread, the extra fee: that is an insurance premium, and the broker has done the actuarial work. **It is willing to write the policy precisely because it knows the kind of market an ordinary stop cannot survive is coming sooner or later.** The premium is this chapter's certainty, quoted at market.

* * *

Push this certainty downward and you get three corollaries.

First, do the risk arithmetic on the assumption that the stop fails, not on the stop distance. "The most I can lose on this trade is 2 percent" holds only if the stop fills at its price, and that premise is precisely the half of the deal that is uncertain. The real question is: if the fill comes in ten times further out than the stop, is my account still here? Position size has to make the answer yes. A stop governs your routine losses; only size governs survival—and there is a chapter later that does this arithmetic properly.

Second, find the two lines of fine print on your account. Does your broker give you negative balance protection? Does your regulator require it? The debts run up by Novak and the people like him are the direct reason Europe and Australia later made negative balance protection compulsory for retail clients—but not every jurisdiction and not every account type has that floor underneath it. Nobody reads those two lines in a good market. The best time to read them was the day you opened the account. The second best is today.

Third, understand the stop as an instrument of discipline, not of protection. What it reliably does is execute, on your behalf, the decision that at this level I was wrong. It guarantees that you leave. It guarantees nothing about the price at which you leave. Traders who see this move the burden of disaster protection off the stop level and onto size and leverage. Traders who do not are the ones who rest an order at 1.19 and then sleep like a man with a sovereign guarantee.

Before that morning, EUR/CHF was the least volatile and most "certain" pair in the market. After it, every trader still standing remembered the same thing: **the trigger is a promise, the fill is luck—and anyone who stakes his survival on luck only gets to lose once.**

(End of Chapter Two)

Chapter Three

A Straight Line, Three Milliseconds Long

Certainty 3: A price difference between brokers will not persist above the cost of arbitrage—and a price difference below the cost of arbitrage can persist forever.

In the spring of 2009, some two thousand men began digging a tunnel across the eastern United States.

The work ran west out of New Jersey, through the Allegheny Mountains of Pennsylvania, straight at Chicago: more than eight hundred miles. The men did not know who was paying them. They knew the money was good, and they knew two rules: don't ask, and report any outsider who does. People living along the route assumed it was a secret government project—nothing else made sense. Pennsylvania, Ohio and Indiana were already laced with fiber underground, all of it perfectly serviceable. Who spends three hundred million dollars to dig one more line?

The answer: a group of traders. And the entire value of that three-hundred-million-dollar cable came down to a single property—**it was straight.** The old routes wandered along railways and highways; this one went through the mountains, near enough a straight line between two points. A signal's round trip fell from 16 milliseconds to 13.

Three hundred million dollars for three milliseconds. Three milliseconds is about one-fiftieth of a blink.

Worth it? The economics explain themselves. Chicago trades the index futures, New York trades the component stocks—one basket of assets, two sets of prices. At any instant the two are a hair out of line, and whoever sees it first can buy on one side and sell on the other simultaneously, pocket the difference, and carry no risk at all. This is not forecasting. It is haulage: **the same object is marked at two prices in two places, and the money belongs to whoever gets there first.** Spread Networks, which built the line, estimated that Wall Street was taking about twenty billion dollars a year out of the gap between New York and Chicago. When the route opened, capacity was priced in the tens of millions, and the industry's verdict came in one sentence: any firm doing business in both cities either took the line or got out of the business.

That is only half the story. The real second half is this: **the cable was arbitraged away in its turn.** Light in glass fiber travels at two-thirds of its speed in a vacuum; through air, at very nearly the full speed of light. Two years after the fiber went live, competitors put up a chain of microwave towers—data flying in a straight line through the sky—and the round trip fell from 13 milliseconds to 10, to 9, to 8.5, and finally to 8.1. The three-hundred-million-dollar straight line through the mountains became, overnight, the slow route. In 2017 Spread Networks was sold for $127 million, less than half what it had cost to build.

* * *

The chapter's certainty is inside that story, and it comes in two complete halves.

The first half: a price difference larger than the cost of arbitrage does not persist. A price difference is unowned money, and unowned money gets taken. That is not a moral judgment, it is the physics of self-interest. The more people chase it and the faster they run, the shorter its life: minutes in the age of the telegraph, milliseconds in the age of fiber, microseconds in the age of microwave. Any quote difference you can see between two brokers, if it is wide enough to cover the spread, the commission and the latency risk, will be eaten by a machine before you have finished noticing it. This half everybody knows.

The second half is the one that gets overlooked: a price difference smaller than the cost of arbitrage can persist forever. Closing a gap costs money—the cable, the towers, the colocation rack, the fee on every fill. When the gap is smaller than those costs, taking it is a losing business, so nobody takes it, so it stays where it is. That is why two brokers' quotes are always a hair apart: the hair lives in the shadow of arbitrage cost, and it is perfectly safe there. **The market does not eliminate mispricing. It eliminates profitable mispricing.** Arbitrage cost draws a boundary. Outside it, nothing grows. Inside it, anything goes.

There is a third layer, hidden in the ending: **the profit of the men who close the gaps does not escape being closed either.** Whoever gets there first gets paid, so everyone races, so the speed advantage itself is priced by competition—the three-hundred-million-dollar line is retired by microwave towers, and the towers then shave milliseconds off one another. This certainty is self-enforcing: it hires the profit-seekers to enforce it, then uses the same profit-seeking to grind their profits away. Retail traders have met another version of the same thing. In the early years there really were people making money on latency arbitrage, running half a step ahead of a slow broker's quotes. The brokers' answer was not to get faster. It was to rewrite the client agreement, bolt on a plugin that rejected the orders, and show those accounts the door. **When your counterparty is also the rule-maker, the price difference disappears by a more direct route**—a subject with a chapter of its own further on.

* * *

Push this certainty downward and you get three corollaries.

First, free money you can see is, by default, money whose costs you have not finished counting. Any price difference visible to the naked eye on a screen and still alive after a second admits three explanations. It is smaller than the full cost and not worth taking. It contains costs you have not counted—latency, rejection, slippage, counterparty risk. Or the other side has the right to change the rules after you win. In all three cases the correct action is the same: nothing. By the time a genuine arbitrage is visible to you, it had long since stopped being one.

Second, quote differences between brokers are the normal state of the world, not a signal. Two platforms a few pips apart tell you nothing about manipulation; it tells you those few pips are living in the cost shadow. The practical meaning lies elsewhere. If you backtest on data from broker A and execute live at broker B, that hair of difference at the edge where your signal triggers is a hidden cost in your system—a system whose data source and execution venue disagree is flipping a coin at every marginal signal.

Third, know the scale at which the gaps get closed and you know which battlefield is yours. The arms race has scrubbed the millisecond scale clean, which means the millisecond battlefield belongs to players who can write a three-hundred-million-dollar check. But arbitrageurs only haul price differences; they take no view. However fast their machines, they will not touch the question of whether the next hour goes up or down. The winners of the speed war make the money of closing gaps. Everyone who cannot win the speed war has to make some other money. Where the other money is, is the subject of the back half of this book.

The straight line dug for three milliseconds is still buried in the body of the Alleghenies, having changed hands more than once for less than half of what it cost. It closed other people's gaps, and then a faster wave closed it. **This certainty owes nobody any favors—least of all its most faithful servants.**

(End of Chapter Three)

Chapter Four

The Green Square

Certainty 4: Cost is locked in as a negative the instant the position opens. Nothing on the revenue side is certain at all.

A ROULETTE WHEEL IS DIVIDED INTO THIRTY-SEVEN SQUARES.

Eighteen red, eighteen black; pick right and your money doubles. It looks like an even game. What makes the house unbeatable is the thirty-seventh square—the green zero. Its presence twists the expected value of every bet negative: not by much, only 2.7 percent, gentle enough to be almost imperceptible. Gamblers study the patterns of red and black, the rhythm of hot numbers and cold, systems for staking, generation after generation. The green square studies nobody. It is simply present in every spin. The palaces of Monte Carlo and the whole length of the Las Vegas Strip stand on this one square—**the house never needs to predict the outcome of a single spin. It needs only certainty on its side, and then it waits for the count to accumulate.**

Most traders have heard the story, and are quite sure they are the ones sitting on the house's side of the table.

So let us make a trade. The most ordinary trade there is: EUR/USD, buy one standard lot, €100,000 notional. Click Buy.

Filled. Now, before you look at the chart, look at the position line.

The trade is already losing.

The price has not moved a tick and you are down. You bought at the ask and you will have to sell at the bid, and the spread sits between them; add the commission on the way in and the way out, and the round-trip cost on a typical retail account comes to about one pip—ten dollars. Ten dollars on a hundred thousand: it sounds like loose change. But notice what kind of number it is. **Those ten dollars are not a risk. They are a constant.** Your target may be reached or it may not. Your direction may be right or wrong. Those ten dollars were paid in full the instant you clicked Buy, and whatever happens afterward, they are not coming back. Of all the cash flows in a trade, the only certain one is the one flowing out.

If you do not close the same day, swap starts accruing by the day—a second cost engine, intricate enough to deserve a chapter of its own, and it will get one. This chapter dissects the single cut made at the moment of entry.

Ten dollars a cut. Hardly worth mentioning. Then let the count speak—that is what the old hands in the casino teach.

Suppose your system is symmetrical, target and stop both twenty pips. Ignore costs and a coin flip breaks even: a 50 percent win rate, nothing gained and nothing lost. Now put that one pip of cost back in. A winner nets nineteen pips; a loser costs twenty-one. The win rate needed to break even becomes 52.5 percent. **Before you have studied a single chart, you are already 2.5 percentage points of win rate in debt**—almost exactly the 2.7 percent of the roulette wheel's green square. The only difference is that the casino paints its green square green, while in your position line it is disguised as a negative number too small to be worth mentioning.

Now let frequency speak. Two hundred trades a year, one lot each, and the costs come to two thousand dollars—on a hundred-thousand-dollar account, a certain 2 percent going out the door every year. Note the grade of certainty on that figure. Your annual return is an unknown; it can be positive or negative and nobody can promise you either. That 2 percent was locked the moment you decided to make two hundred trades a year: rain or shine, direction irrelevant. **For most traders it is the only number of the year certain to be delivered.**

* * *

PUSH THIS CERTAINTY DOWNWARD AND YOU GET THREE COROLLARIES.

First, expected value must be computed net, or you are paying yourself an imaginary bonus. A backtest without costs is practicing your craft on a wheel with no green square—however good you get, the real table finds you out. A strategy that is gross-positive and net-negative can print a very handsome equity curve in testing and will certainly die live, and it will die slowly, slowly enough that you spend the whole time believing the problem is your execution. The first judgment on any system is not whether it can make money. It is whether its gross edge is large enough to feed the costs first.

Second, cost is the only certain compounding in the account, and frequency is its only valve. On the revenue side you control nothing. On the cost side you control the largest variable there is: how many times you trade. With the same edge, cut half of the trades you could take or leave, and every dollar of cost you save is real money. This is not patience-is-a-virtue counseling, it is cost accounting: **trading less is not self-restraint, it is a direct source of profit.** Conversely, anything that pushes your frequency up—the signal alert, the intraday push notification, the itch that says here comes the opportunity—is out touting for the green square.

Third, the ratio of cost to edge decides which time frame you can live in. One pip of cost against a swing trade targeting a hundred pips is 1 percent, effectively invisible. Against a scalp targeting five pips it is 20 percent—a fifth of the profit taxed away at the moment of entry. The shorter the holding period, the more of your table the green square occupies. This is why the bodies pile so much higher in short-term trading than in long: most scalpers do not die of direction, they die of the tax rate. They take a game that was roughly even and turn it into a charitable donation to the house. Your holding period has to shrink cost to loose change against expected profit, and that piece of arithmetic comes before every technical consideration in choosing one.

The genius of the casino was never in winning a particular spin; it has no interest whatever in any particular spin. It simply makes sure the green square is present at every turn of the wheel, and leaves the undignified work of predicting the future to the people across the table. In the market, the spread and the commission are that square. The one difference from the casino is this: **how many times the wheel spins is up to you.**

(End of Chapter Four)

Chapter Five

Five O'Clock on Wednesday

Certainty 5: The moment swap is charged is certain. The cost calendar is hard—including that strange triple day.

June 26, 1974. Cologne. Half past four in the afternoon.

Officials of the German regulator walked into Herstatt Bank, revoked its license on the spot, and ordered it wound up. The bank had lost 470 million marks on speculative dollar positions against total capital of 44 million—a hole more than ten times its own money. Closing a bank that has gambled and lost is routine supervision. What put this particular day into financial history was a detail nobody had thought twice about: **the hour of the closure.**

Half past four in Cologne was half past ten in the morning in New York. That same morning, several international banks, settling foreign exchange trades agreed with Herstatt, had paid it marks in Frankfurt—by convention the corresponding dollars would come back to their accounts a few hours later, inside New York business hours. The marks went out. The license was revoked. The dollars never arrived. The counterparties were left clutching unsecured claims against a bankrupt bank, and what they lost was **the entire principal**—not a price difference, the principal. Some $200 million of trades hung in mid-air, panic ran out through the correspondent-banking network worldwide, and the interbank market froze. The Basel Committee was founded at the Bank for International Settlements because of it, and the settlement system that finally sealed the hole was not built for another twenty-eight years.

What that accident tore open is the floorboard the foreign exchange market normally keeps best hidden: **a currency trade is not one action but two payments—in two time zones, hours apart.** On the screen, price is instantaneous. Money is not. Money travels through real plumbing, and plumbing keeps a calendar of its own.

Look down through that floor and the line in your account that moves every day—swap—stops being mysterious.

* * *

THE "SPOT" FOREIGN EXCHANGE YOU TRADE ON A PLATFORM IS NOT, by global convention, spot at all: it settles on the **second business day** after the trade, T+2 in the jargon. That convention is a direct inheritance from Herstatt's era—two time zones, two clearing systems, and confirmation and transfer take time. But neither you nor your broker has the slightest intention of actually delivering ten million euros, so every day at five o'clock New York time the system rolls your position over: it closes the leg settling today and rebuilds the identical position, at the same price, settling tomorrow. In price, your position has not moved a hair. On the calendar, it has moved back one day.

And moving the calendar costs interest. Because holding a currency pair is, in substance, **holding two loans at once**: long EUR/USD means borrowing dollars and lending euros—you collect interest on the euros, you pay interest on the dollars, and the difference between the two, plus the broker's cut, is the line of swap that crosses your account at five o'clock. It is not a commission and not a penalty. It is the real interest differential on those two loans, positive or negative with the two countries' rates—which is also why the same instrument carries a different swap long and short, and why sometimes you pay and sometimes the market pays you.

Now the famous riddle can be opened. **Why is Wednesday charged three times?**

Work it out on the calendar. Roll at five o'clock on Wednesday and your value date moves from Friday to the next business day—Saturday and Sunday do not settle, so the next business day is **Monday**. The calendar moved one day; the value date jumped three. Three days of funding, three days of interest, settled in one stroke. So Wednesday's triple is not the rule being capricious. It is the rule being exact: **that is the weekend's interest, collected two days early, on Wednesday's bill**—because of T+2, the Wednesday position is the one holding the loan across the weekend.

A careful reader will press: trades done on Thursday and Friday have value dates that must also step over the weekend, so why are they not tripled? Spread the calendar out and count day by day and it comes clear. Trade on Thursday and the value date is the following Monday—Friday is the first business day, skip the weekend, Monday is the second. Roll that position overnight on Thursday and the value date moves to Tuesday: Monday to Tuesday, **one day** of movement, one day of interest. Trade on Friday and the value date is Tuesday; roll it and the value date moves to Wednesday—one day again. The weekend does appear in both of those accounts, but only as a gap stepped over in the **calculation** of the value date, and swap charges only for **movement** of the value date. Only in Wednesday's rollover does the movement itself land on the weekend: Friday straight through to Monday, three real days. Then look at Saturday and Sunday: the market is shut, there is no rollover to perform, so nothing is charged. Add the week up—one, one, three, one, one. **Seven days exactly, not a fraction more.** Wednesday does not overcharge you; it collects on the weekend's behalf. Over a year you pay one day per day, three hundred and sixty-five of them. A mechanism that closes its own books that neatly has earned your belief that there is no caprice behind it, only rules. By the same logic, when a bank holiday falls on the settlement path, swap is deferred and multiplied to match. The whole apparatus meshes like clockwork—and every gear in that clock is engraved in the published contract specifications.

Do not, however, learn the slogan by heart. Gold is usually T+2 as well and most brokers triple it on Wednesday too, but there are exceptions; index CFDs commonly triple on Friday; crypto is another species entirely—it trades through the weekend and settles instantly, so swap is charged seven days a week, there is no triple day, and the rate is often negative in both directions and a great deal more expensive. **What is certain is not the slogan "triple on Wednesday." What is certain is that every instrument's cost calendar is set down in black and white in the contract specifications, checkable years in advance.** Slogans expire. Specifications do not.

* * *

Push this certainty downward and three corollaries follow.

First, swap is the only bill in the whole market that says out loud that you are borrowing money. Leverage sounds like a multiplier the platform is making you a present of; swap reminds you what it really is—an interest-bearing loan. From which: the expected value of any overnight strategy has to include this daily drip. A position that is right on direction but negative on carry surrenders more of its profit the longer you hold it; on a swing trade held two weeks, total swap can easily exceed spread and commission combined. The last chapter said cost is locked at the instant you open. This chapter adds the second half: **as long as you hold overnight, cost is locked again every day.**

Second, one calendar, two businesses. Some people study this calendar in order to dodge it—close intraday, never hold overnight, swap goes to zero. That is the last chapter's "frequency is the valve on cost," applied to the dimension of the calendar. Others study it in order to earn from it: borrow the low-yielding currency, hold the high-yielding one, and let the differential drip into your account day after day. This is the carry trade, an entire school built on that one line of swap. The calendar plays no favorites; it rewards only those who have read it. And the Japanese retail traders detonated in layers during the flash crash of January 3, 2019 were in precisely this business—**earning the calendar's money and losing their lives to the volatility**—a relationship this book will settle the full account on in a later chapter.

Third, the fine print has to be reread every year. A swap rate is not a constant of nature; it is a price quoted by your broker. It can be changed, and historically it has been changed continually, with notice that is often one line of small type on a website. The rate you verified three years ago may no longer be the rate. Which opens a larger subject—who holds the power to interpret the rules and to change them. That is Chapter Nine's proper business; here we only plant a marker.

Herstatt failed, incidentally, on a Wednesday. The interbank hole took twenty-eight years to fill, and the T+2 gearing still turns beneath your platform—every day at five o'clock New York time it reminds you, on schedule: **price is instantaneous; money is not. Behind every quote you see, real money is trekking through a calendar two days out—and swap is the toll for that gap in time.**

(End of Chapter Five)

Chapter Six

The Partner Who Never Loses

Certainty 6: Tax is certain, and it is asymmetric—levied only on profits; losses can only be carried forward, never refunded in cash.

Start with two years of accounts.

A trader makes $100,000 in his first year. At a rate of 30% he pays $30,000 in tax. In the second year the market turns on him and he loses $100,000. Across the two years his trading career is a draw: not a cent made, not a cent lost.

Now look at his bank account: **down $30,000.**

The first year's tax, once paid, is paid. Against the second year's loss, nobody refunds him a penny. The tax authority arrives punctually in the years he makes money and takes its three tenths; in the years he loses money it is nowhere to be found and carries none of it. Two years to a wash, and after tax the result is solidly negative—and that $30,000 was not lost by getting the direction wrong. It was taken by **structure**.

That is this chapter's certainty, ordinarily hidden in the forms of tax season, and one sentence says the whole of it: **you have a partner who takes part in every profit and never in a loss.** Every hand you win, he is at the table for his share. Every hand you lose, he happens to be out of the room. If anyone proposed that split to you in a card game you would turn the table over on the spot; in real trading the split is not open to negotiation, is written into law, and executes itself.

Someone will object: not so—losses can be carried forward and offset against later profits. Correct, and this is exactly where the magnifying glass belongs. **A carryforward is not a refund. It is an IOU**—and a carefully designed one. It pays no interest. It cannot be cashed. Its only means of redemption is that you **win again** later, using future profit to write off past loss. Which is to say it becomes valuable only when you no longer need it: if you rise again, it saves you some tax; if you never recover, it goes to zero along with your account. **The year you need cash most is precisely the year that IOU is worth least.** Some jurisdictions give the screw another turn: in the United States, capital losses can be deducted against ordinary income at only $3,000 a year—a $100,000 loss, absorbed against a salary, would take more than thirty years. The IOU pays no interest, and it lets you tear off only one small corner at a time.

If that still sounds abstract, the crypto market of 2021 and 2022 supplied a whole casebook. In November 2021 Bitcoin touched above $68,000, and countless traders had spent that year buying and selling and had booked considerable realized gains—then rolled the profits into new positions. In 2022 the market broke below $20,000 and the gains went up in smoke; a still unluckier group had their assets frozen inside bankrupt platforms and could not withdraw at all. Then tax season came. The rules ground on, cold: **the gains realized in 2021 are on the record, and the tax is due**—how much money you have left today falls outside the calculation. Accounts down ninety percent received bills computed on a peak year's record. People whose entire holdings were frozen by a platform still owed tax on what those holdings had "earned" them the day before. The tax authority cuts your trading life into calendar years—**and the market has never agreed to settle by the calendar year.** The misalignment between those two systems of time runs over a fresh batch of people every few years, and every batch believes it is the first.

Push one layer deeper and the asymmetry conceals a more discreet toll booth: **tax is a second levy on volatility.** Two traders with identical pre-tax profit over ten years—one grinding out a small steady gain year after year, the other alternating large gains with large losses. The steady one settles every year at a low burden; the volatile one is taxed heavily in the winning years while his deductions from the losing years are deferred, shrunk, or left hanging forever. At the ten-year mark, two curves that are identical before tax differ by a visible margin after it. **The total of gains and losses is the same; only the order of their arrival differs—and the wealth differs.** So after-tax expectancy is emphatically not pre-tax expectancy multiplied by (1 − tax rate). That formula assumes symmetry, and symmetry is exactly what the tax code does not contain.

* * *

PUSH THIS CERTAINTY DOWNWARD AND THREE COROLLARIES follow.

First, evaluating a system requires an after-tax measure. Of two systems perfectly equivalent before tax, the one with lower volatility and a smoother profit stream is worth more after tax—not more comfortable psychologically, more valuable arithmetically. Later in this book we will watch volatility charge you a first time, through the arithmetic of compounding; here it charges you a second time, through the tax code. Every unit of effort spent suppressing volatility pays out on both sets of books.

Second, the carryforward IOU cannot be booked as an asset. In a risk budget, a losing year's loss counts in full—nobody is sharing it; a winning year's profit counts only after tax—the partner will certainly attend. From which a further discipline follows: **in a profitable year, the tax money should come off the table within the year.** This year's bill is not forgiven by next year's loss, and a trader who keeps opening positions with tax he has not yet remitted is, in substance, adding size with his partner's money—and this partner has never accepted "I lost it all" as grounds for non-payment.

Third, residence is a trading parameter, and one of the kind that takes effect before the race begins. Jurisdictions differ enormously in how they characterize trading gains: capital gain or business income, at what rate, how losses are treated, whether holding period changes the rate—all of it in black and white, all of it checkable in advance. Two identical traders in two countries can have after-tax curves with two different faces. This book offers no tax advice; it points out only a fact commonly ignored: **part of your after-tax return was settled on the day you moved into a particular country**—a parameter that deserves to be compared as carefully as you compare spreads, and most people spend a hundred times longer on the spreads.

Back to the trader from the opening, two years flat and $30,000 out of pocket. His error lies in no single trade—every trade he can review, criticize, improve. That $30,000 has nowhere to be reviewed, because it did not come from the market. It came from structure. **This is the distinction the chapter means to fix: money lost to the market's uncertainty is**

at least forgivable; money lost to structure is lost entirely to clauses written in advance, which anyone may read free of charge. And the partner who never loses is turning the pages of his calendar at this moment, waiting for your next profitable year.

(End of Chapter Six)

Chapter Seven

Money on Someone Else's Books

Certainty 7: Until you withdraw it, your account balance is your broker's liability, not your property.

October 31, 2011. Halloween. Half past two in the morning.

Officials of the U.S. Commodity Futures Trading Commission had been working straight through the weekend. MF Global, an old-line broker, had a $6.3 billion position in European sovereign debt that had dragged the firm to the cliff edge, and the regulatory plan was the industry-standard move: before the bankruptcy, transfer tens of thousands of customer accounts, margin and all, in one block to another broker—a painless handover, positions not even closed. A receiving firm had been agreed. The documents were prepared.

At half past two, one message ended all of it: **the segregated client funds did not reconcile, and the shortfall was enormous.** The acquirer withdrew on the spot—no broker will take on a pile of positions that lack their margin. Hours later MF Global filed for bankruptcy, the eighth largest in American history. As the liquidation opened up, the full shape of the hole surfaced: about $1.6 billion of customer money missing.

A word has to be explained here: **segregation**. The client-money rules of the U.S. futures industry are among the strictest in the world—customer money must sit in accounts entirely separate from the firm's own funds, and the broker may not put it to any use of its own. That is iron law, written into federal regulation. MF Global's customers, among them a great many farmers and ranchers hedging a harvest with futures, believed in that wall. What the liquidation trustee later established was this: in the firm's final days, to meet its own margin calls and overdrafts, it wired money out of the segregated customer accounts, transfer by transfer, to its own banks and counterparties. How disordered were the books? The shortfall had existed since at least Wednesday, and the firm itself did not discover it until Friday. **The wall was not knocked down. The men guarding it took it apart to fight a fire.**

The ending is often offered as consolation: after the liquidation, customers got all their money back in the end. But look closely at the grade of that "in the end"—**it took more than two years.** For two years, hedging farmers watched their positions liquidated and their exposure run naked into the market; traders who needed margin scrambled for money elsewhere; every man's "balance" became a claim filed in a bankruptcy court. And the executives who presided over the whole thing, after congressional hearings and litigation, bore no criminal liability, not one of them. What the customers won back was money that had been theirs all along—**and in that victory there was no interest.**

* * *

WHAT THIS CASE TORE OPEN IS THE LEGAL BEDROCK BENEATH EVERY trader's account screen, and it can be said in a single sentence: **the moment you deposit, your money stops being yours.**

You wire $10,000 to your broker. That $10,000 enters its bank account and becomes an asset on its balance sheet; on the other side it records a line under liabilities: owes you $10,000. The "balance" you see on the platform is the display interface for that liability—**what you hold is not a deposit but a claim; not property, but somebody else's written promise.** Your open profit makes the liability larger, your withdrawal makes it smaller, and its redeemability depends, always, on the survival of the company on the other side of the ledger.

Segregation rules, trust accounts, compensation schemes—these are real, and really useful, but see their legal nature clearly. **They are protective layers laid over that claim. They improve the quality of the claim; they cannot change what it is.** Segregation is an accounting operation performed by the debtor itself, and MF Global proved it can give way at the one moment that matters. Compensation schemes have caps, conditions, and differences by jurisdiction. And across most corners of the global retail foreign exchange and CFD industry, client-money rules are a great deal looser than that American iron law. The protective layers exist, layer upon layer, and every layer has holes—this is not alarmism; it is what each layer's own text says of itself.

As for "pick a big platform and you're safe"—MF Global was run by a former head of Goldman Sachs and former state governor, and was among the largest brokers on several global exchanges. Size and prestige are adjectives describing a debtor. **What a creditor should care about has only ever been one thing: whose books the money is on.**

* * *

Push this certainty downward and three corollaries follow.

First, withdrawal is the last step in the manufacture of a profit, not an optional habit. A trade does not close its loop at the moment you exit the position, but at the moment the money lands back in your bank account. Everything made before that has one legal identity: appreciation of a claim. From which withdrawal frequency ought to be, like a stop, an explicitly specified parameter of the system—move the profits off someone else's books and onto your own, on a schedule. However beautiful the equity curve on the platform, what it records is the history of an IOU, and the final value of an IOU is decided by whether it gets paid.

Second, your broker is your single largest counterparty; manage it as one. You cap risk at 2% on a trade and keep 100% of your capital at one broker. As a risk budget the combination is absurd, only so common that the absurdity goes unnoticed. Spreading funds across several regulated platforms is not fussiness, it is elementary counterparty diversification; and studying a jurisdiction's client-money regime and compensation cap before you open an account is worth ten times the hours you would put into an indicator setting.

Third, read the "client money" clause in your account agreement, once, all the way through. This is the third time this book has walked you to the fine print: Chapter Two was the negative-balance clause, Chapter Five the swap rate schedule, this chapter the client money terms—how your money is held, which queue you stand in at insolvency, how far the compensation scheme reaches. The three sets of small type have one thing in common. **The best time to read them is the day you open the account, and the second best is today; the time most people choose is the day of the accident—by which point they have stopped being terms and become a verdict.**

After that Halloween morning the U.S. futures industry patched its rules, barring customer funds from a number of high-risk uses. The wall went up a course higher. But the nature of the wall has not changed: **what it protects is still a claim, and the other end of a claim is always tied to somebody else's books.** The number in your platform will light up on time again tonight, accurate to two decimal places—precision is the expression it wears best. Whether it is worth that much has never been answered on the screen.

(End of Chapter Seven)

Chapter Eight

The Evening Eraser

Certainty 8: A price that has traded cannot be changed. The record of it can.

May 6, 2010. 2:40 p.m., New York time.

Accenture—a consulting firm worth more than thirty billion dollars—was trading around $40, as on any of a thousand ordinary afternoons. Then, over the next few minutes, the American market went through the thirty-six minutes later known as the Flash Crash: the Dow fell nearly a thousand points, a trillion dollars of market value evaporated into air, and most of it came back before the close. On Accenture's tape there printed a price of **one cent**; seven other stocks in the S&P 500 also traded at a penny; and Sotheby's tape ran up to **something near $100,000**. Where those absurd numbers came from would make a chapter of its own—with market makers pulling their quotes en masse, the stub quotes resting deep in the order book, extreme limit orders left there as jokes or as placeholders, became the only counterparties left in the market, and incoming market orders drove straight into them and filled, one by one.

Note the word "traded." These were not quotes, not an illusion. They were **completed transactions**—there was a buyer, there was a seller, money changed hands, and Accenture at a penny was bought with real money.

Then evening came.

After the close, representatives of the exchanges and the regulators met. The item on the agenda: which part of that afternoon should **be deleted from history**. After what official testimony would later call "extended discussion," they drew a line—every trade executed more than **60%** away from its 2:40 p.m. reference price was void, deemed never to have happened. More than twenty thousand trades, 5.5 million shares, erased as a batch that evening; Nasdaq alone "broke" 10,468 of them. And where did that 60% line come from? The testimony is candid: it was argued out in the room—Nasdaq wanted only trades beyond 80% canceled, other institutions wanted 50%, and the compromise settled at 60. The official report afterward conceded that the number had produced a "list of winners and losers," and that the basis for the list was **arbitrary**.

How arbitrary? A trader whose stop was triggered and filled 59% down keeps the loss and has nowhere to appeal; his neighbor, filled 61% down, has the trade voided and is resurrected where he stood. And a group who had stepped in during the collapse to take the other side, and had made money, had their winning fills erased along with the rest—they protested that they were the ones supplying liquidity in a crash, so on what grounds were they being punished? On no grounds. **That afternoon, the market decided the prices. That evening, a conference room decided which prices counted.**

The most interesting part is a data ghost. For a long time afterward, Accenture's "52-week low" showed in some records as $17.74—a price from May 6 that officially never happened, still drifting in a corner of the database. **Even the erasure did not erase cleanly.**

* * *

THIS CHAPTER'S CERTAINTY SPLITS, ACCORDINGLY, INTO TWO STRICT halves.

The first half is hard: **an execution is a physical fact.** At the instant that penny-priced Accenture was bought, money really moved between buyer and seller. That happened, and no later resolution can alter the fact that it happened.

The second half is the chapter's real subject. **The "history" you read when you backtest is not that physical fact. It is a record maintained by human beings—and the maintainers hold an eraser.** The Flash Crash was only the eraser's most theatrical appearance; its everyday work is far quieter, and most of it is not even called scandal. It is called data maintenance.

Every time a stock goes ex-dividend, the adjustment algorithm rewrites **the entire price history**—the candle on your chart from ten years ago has quietly changed value because of a dividend paid last month. The "continuous contract" stitched together across futures rollovers contains long stretches of price that are mathematical construction and never traded in any market. Brokers repair bad prints after the fact and backfill missing ticks. Vendors' cleaning routines delete "outliers"—and May 6 proved that some outliers are real trades. Delisted stocks vanish from the database entire, so a backtest run on current index constituents counts, by construction, only the winners that survived to today. The same strategy over the same stretch of history, fed data from two vendors, produces two different equity curves—and the divergence concentrates precisely where signals trigger, and deep inside extreme conditions.

* * *

PUSH THIS CERTAINTY DOWNWARD AND THREE COROLLARIES follow.

First, every backtest conclusion is bound to a version of the data, the way an experimental result is bound to its instrument. You rerun the same backtest six months later and the result has changed—suspect that the data was revised before you suspect that the strategy has decayed. Both are possible, but most people think only of the second, and so they kill or trust their system on the evidence of a curve contaminated by a data change. The serious practice is plain to the point of clumsiness: record the data source and the date you obtained it; and for the strategies most sensitive to data—short holding periods, tight stops—cross-check the whole thing against a second vendor. The gap between the two curves is the error bar on your backtest.

Second, forward live trading is the only verification whose version you control. The signals, fills, and slippage you record yourself in real time, stamped with the moment they landed, will not be revised afterward by any vendor—because the person maintaining them is you. Which lays the foundation under a position this book keeps returning to: the backtest is only the first hearing, the forward test is the final one—not merely because forward data cannot be overfitted, but because **forward data is the only history in front of you guaranteed untouched by the eraser**. Your own system, your own database, line by line: it is one of the few things on this market you genuinely own.

Third, the more extreme the historical data, the less it can be trusted—and that is exactly where you need it most. Stress testing calls for historical extremes, and historical extremes are the very stretch where the eraser is busiest: the canceled fills, the "bad prints" scrubbed away, the gaps smoothed flat by adjustment. The worst case you read out of the data is usually a worst case that has been tidied; **the real abyss is deeper than the archived one**. Build that discount into your stress-test parameters, and while you are there remember May 6's other lesson: even your own executions on the day can have their validity changed by an evening meeting—**strictly speaking, your live P&L is not final until other people have gone home**. Who holds the power to interpret the rules is the next chapter's direct business.

A price chart looks like a fossil—ancient, hard, beyond dispute. Its real texture is closer to the online edition of a dictionary: broadly reliable, maintained over the long run, editable forever, with an edit history that is not shown to you. **Fossils don't lie. The liars are the people who file them—and they never even have to lie. All they have to do is "maintain."**

(End of Chapter Eight)

Chapter Nine

The Eight Hours That Never Happened

Certainty 9: Certainty on the rule side is maintained unilaterally—whoever writes the rules can rewrite them at any time, and you have no vote.

March 8, 2022. London, before dawn.

Twelve days after the war in Ukraine began, the price of nickel on the London Metal Exchange was leaving the earth's gravity. On March 7 it rose 69% in a single session, closing near $50,000 a tonne; before dawn on the 8th it kept climbing, and by six in the morning it had broken **$100,000**—a double in five hours, driven by a textbook short squeeze. A mining giant's enormous short book had been backed into a corner, and the covering bids were trampling the price upward.

Suppose you were long that morning. You may have been holding the move of a generation, and every fill you had was real, lawful, matched under the rules of the exchange.

At 8:15 a.m., the LME suspended nickel trading. At 12:05 p.m., the notice went out: **every nickel trade done that day before the suspension was canceled.** Eight hours, roughly twelve billion dollars of turnover, declared not to have happened. The market then closed and did not reopen for a week. The large player the squeeze had driven to the edge of default was saved; the winners on the other side watched their profits go to zero—not handed back. **Never made.**

This time the party on the other side was not a retail trader. The hedge fund Elliott and the market maker Jane Street—two of the most rule-literate institutions on earth—sued the LME jointly for $472 million, arguing that the exchange had no power to void lawful trades and that its decision amounted, in substance, to a bailout of a dying short. The case ran two and a half years. The chain of rulings went like this: the High Court dismissed the claim; the Court of Appeal upheld the dismissal, and wrote its reasoning in plain sight—Rule 22 of the LME rulebook grants the exchange the power to cancel trades in a "disorderly market," and the judges went out of their way to note that **the cancellation power is itself part of what the regulators require**, a lawful instrument kept ready for extreme moments; the Supreme Court refused permission to appeal, finding no point of law worth arguing. Read that literally: the matter was not even worth discussing.

There is a footnote, too, ironic in a way no novelist would dare: in 2025 the Financial Conduct Authority formally found the LME at fault on several counts that night—including the fact that in the pre-dawn hours when the price ran out of control, the only people on duty were junior staff with no authority to act. **The referee was officially found derelict. The score stands.**

The sharpest splinter is buried in a corner of the judgment. Elliott was not even an LME member. It had never signed anything with the exchange. But the court held that through its contracts with members it had "incorporated" the whole of the LME rulebook—Rule 22, and its capacity to wake up, included.

You never signed the rules; the rules bind you anyway. Inside every contract you did sign, nested one layer down, is somebody else's rulebook that you have not read.

* * *

If this strikes you as a modern disease, turn the calendar back forty-two years.

In 1979 the Hunt brothers—Texas oil money—concluded that inflation would devour the dollar and poured the family fortune into silver, cornering, with allies, a substantial share of the world's deliverable metal. Silver went from six dollars an ounce to nearly fifty by January 1980. Their thesis was right. Their position was right. Their timing was right.

Then the rules moved. On January 7, 1980, Comex issued Silver Rule 7, sharply tightening position limits; two weeks later came the kill shot: **the silver market was placed on a liquidation-only basis, effective immediately**—everyone could sell, no one could open a new long. In a market where the only permitted trade is a sale, price has one direction. Silver collapsed. On Silver Thursday, March 27, the Hunts failed to meet margin calls of more than a hundred million dollars, and the empire came apart. The record preserves one more detail: several members of the exchange board held short positions in silver themselves. **The men who changed the rules happened to stand on the winning side of the change.** All of it, again, perfectly legal.

Forty-two years, two cases, one script: **when your profit grows large enough to threaten someone the system needs, the thing that gets liquidated is not them. It is the rule that was paying you.** The LME canceled retroactively—erasing what had already happened. Comex amended prospectively—forbidding what was about to. An eraser and a floodgate: two tools in the same hand. Last chapter we established that the eraser exists. This chapter answers who holds it, and what the law makes of that hand—**the answer is that the law looked at it and nodded.**

We can now add the same line of fine print to all eight of the certainties that came before. Trading hours are certain, the stop mechanism is certain, the swap calendar is certain, the tax code is certain, the segregation rules are certain—every one of them real, and every one of them, stated in full, ending: **"for as long as the rule remains in force."** What is certain is that the rule exists, not that it endures. The only clause with no fine print attached is the ownership of the power to amend, and that, with total certainty, does not sit with you. A central bank can pull the floor out from under an exchange rate. A regulator can rewrite the leverage cap overnight. An exchange can cancel your eight hours. And nearly every broker's client agreement carries the sentence: "The Company reserves the right to amend these terms at any time." That sentence is not boilerplate. **That sentence is this chapter, abridged.**

* * *

Pushed downward, this certainty yields three corollaries.

First: whenever you read a rule, find its amendment clause and its exception clause before anything else. What the rule says matters, but what decides your fate is who has the power to make it say something else, and under what conditions. Rule 22 sleeps for years, unread by anyone; on the night of a crisis it wakes and erases twelve billion dollars in a single sentence.

Every agreement you sign houses a few sleepers like it. This is the third fine-print reading list this book has issued, and it ends here with one last item: find the sleeping Rule 22 in your own contract, and memorize its face.

Second: run a rule stress test on your best-case profit. This is the least intuitive corollary in the chapter and the most valuable. The moment a rule is most likely to change is not when you are losing—your losses threaten no one—but **on the day you win biggest**. Because the far side of an extreme profit is usually the extreme loss of someone the system needs, and what rules protect has never been your statement; it is the system's continuity. The official post-mortem put it about as bluntly as it can be put: the cancellation averted the default of a major participant, at a cost of "merely" the speculative profits of financial players. So when your position meets the move of a generation, let something colder ride alongside the euphoria. **Extreme profit carries its own confiscation risk**—at that moment, how fast you book it matters more than how large it is.

Third: the outermost layer of tail-risk management defends against rules, not prices. Extreme prices can be met with position size and stops; extreme rules defeat both—no stop order stops a press release. The only defense is structural: spread capital and positions across exchanges, across brokers, across jurisdictions, so that no single rule-maker's single wave of the hand can reach all of you. And beneath that, a floor: **never let your exit depend on the goodwill of the people who write the rules.**

Part One closes here. Nine certainties, all of them drawn from contracts, ledgers, and clauses—real, checkable, existing before any price move does. And the last of them stamps the other eight: even these certainties come with an expiry clause of their own. **In this market, certainty itself carries fine print.** There is one consolation. One class of certainty lies beyond the reach of any rule-maker: mathematics accepts no amendments. In the next part, we turn to the arithmetic of defense.

(End of Chapter Nine · End of Part One)

Part Two

The Mathematics of Defense

Chapter Ten

A Coin That Keeps Its Word

Certainty 10: Position size is the only variable you control 100%.

2016. An unusual lecture.

Sixty-one invited participants filed in—top students in economics and finance, and young professionals from investment firms, every one of them quantitatively trained. They believed they had come to hear a hedge fund partner share some hard-won lessons. Instead the speaker opened by handing out money: twenty-five real dollars each, a computer, and on the screen an electronic coin that could be flipped. Three rules. **The coin comes up heads 60% of the time—in writing, disclosed in advance.** For the next thirty minutes you may stake whatever you like on whichever side you like. When the thirty minutes are up, whatever remains in the account is written to you as a check, capped at two hundred and fifty dollars.

Stop for three seconds and think about how you would play it. A face-up coin, sixty percent heads, a stake of twenty-five dollars, room for roughly three hundred flips. This is about the kindest gamble on earth: the edge is real, the edge is known, and the edge is printed on the wall.

Now the results. **Twenty-eight percent of them went bust**, losing every cent. A third finished below their starting stake.

The average check came to ninety-one dollars—while a sensible fixed fraction, bet steadily, would have carried almost anyone to the $250 cap. The process data is more frightening than the outcome. Of the sixty-one, **eighteen put their entire bankroll on a single flip**. Two-thirds bet tails at some point—note that this is after being told explicitly that heads runs at sixty percent, and choosing to hand the money to the forty. Nearly half bet tails more than five times. A good number ran a martingale, doubling after losses, rolling small deficits into zero. And a footnote: asked afterward, of sixty-one credentialed players, the number who had ever heard of the Kelly criterion—the mathematics devoted precisely to how much to bet—was **five**.

When it was over, the coin handed in its own report card: 7,253 flips in all, 59.6% heads. **The coin kept every word it had given.** Of the three in ten who died, not one was killed by a lie.

Now the speaker. The man who designed the experiment, Victor Haghani, was a founding partner of Long-Term Capital Management. That LTCM: the legend of 1998, two Nobel laureates on the premises, the finest minds on Wall Street, broadly right about direction, and ground to powder by a brief adverse move at more than twenty times leverage, very nearly taking the global financial system with it. A man who lived through the most expensive position-sizing accident in human history built a miniature of the same accident for the next generation, at twenty-five dollars a ticket. **He knew better than anyone what needed demonstrating: people do not die over whether the edge exists. They die over how much they bet.**

*   *   *

THAT IS THE FIRST CERTAINTY OF PART TWO, AND THE ONLY ONE IN this book that sounds like good news: of all the variables in trading, **exactly one is in your hands, completely, from beginning to end.**

Take the inventory and the weight of that sentence becomes clear. Direction? Not yours—Part One covered it: intent is invisible, the future does not exist yet. Fill price? Not yours—a stop promises only to trigger. Costs? Certain, but certainly flowing outward. Rules? Chapter Nine just stamped that one: the power to amend belongs to someone else. Even the existence of your own edge is something you can infer for a lifetime and never confirm—the market will never do what that coin did and print the probability on the wall for you. But the size box in the order ticket: **from the day you open the account to the day you close it, no person, no price move, and no rule can fill it in for you.** It is the one pure input on the entire machine.

The experiment also proved, in passing, a deeper theorem: **bet size can turn a positive-expectation game into a game you are certain to lose.** A positive expectation guarantees only that you make money on average, and you do not live in the average. You live on one particular path. The larger the fraction you stake, the more violently that path shakes; past a certain size, a few ordinary runs of bad luck are enough to deliver you to zero —and once you are at zero, all the good luck that follows belongs to somebody else. The eighteen who went all in were betting the sixty side. The expectation was plainly positive. Yet two flips is all it takes: four tenths times four tenths, and there is a sixteen percent chance you never flip a third time. **The edge**

sets the slope of the long run. Position size decides whether you reach the long run. Bet a small fixed fraction of capital instead, and what you lose each time is a corner of what remains—mathematically you can never touch absolute zero. That property, geometric decay, is what a position rule gives to survivors.

* * *

PUSHED DOWNWARD, THIS CERTAINTY YIELDS THREE COROLLARIES.

First: build the system in this order—position rules first, entry and exit signals second. Most people go the other way, hunting for the holy grail and sizing by mood. Get the hierarchy right: signals govern the slope, position size governs survival, and survival is a precondition of slope. A mediocre signal with a strict fixed fraction will, at worst, wear out your patience slowly. An excellent signal with a size that floats on your feelings needs only one bad day. The risk engine should be the first module you build and the last one you compromise.

Second: position size is the developer that brings your emotions out, and the rule is the seal on the envelope. Look back at every way people died in that experiment. Going all in is the position-shape of greed. The martingale is the position-shape of revenge. Betting tails is the position-shape of doubting your own system. **Every psychological hole has to come through the one input, the size box, in order to commit its crime.** That structure hands the defense an enormous bargain: you do not have to repair your psychology, which is a life's work. You only have to nail the position rule down—into code, and into a moment before the impulse arrives. The eighteen who went all in probably understood probability perfectly well.

They simply had an impulse, on the spot. The whole value of a rule is that it was signed before the impulse.

Third: buy information with position size. Whether a new system's edge is real or imaginary has one judge only—live forward trading—and forward validation costs money, priced per unit by the single variable you control. Run the minimum size until the sample is large enough, let the statistics develop first, then step up along a ladder written in advance; each rung of size corresponds to a rung of confidence already earned. Treat size as adjustable tuition, not as chips to be played with—**the smaller you bet during validation, the cheaper you buy the same truth.**

The coin was flipped 7,253 times and delivered 59.6% heads—four tenths of a percentage point below what it had promised. The market will never make you a promise of that kind at all. And the three in ten who went bust, holding a luxury that exists in no real market—a known edge, in writing—died in the end of a number that nobody but they had the right to fill in. **The edge was somebody else's gift. The way you die, you write yourself.**

(*End of Chapter Ten*)

Chapter Eleven

The Twenty-Sixth Black

Certainty 11: A drawdown is inevitable—the question is never whether, only when and how deep.

The night of August 18, 1913. The Monte Carlo Casino.

At one roulette table, black began to repeat. By the fifth spin and the sixth, a crowd was forming; by the tenth, players were abandoning other tables to get there; by the fifteenth the crowd stood three deep—and every one of them was doing the same thing: **betting red, and betting bigger each time.** The logic was airtight inside every head in the room. Black has come up this many times, red is "due," and each additional black makes red more due still. The wheel took no notice. Black ran all the way to **the twenty-sixth spin** before red finally landed. When the dust settled, the players had lost francs in the millions. The night went into the textbooks as the naming scene of the gambler's fallacy: the wheel has no memory, and after twenty-five blacks the probability of a twenty-sixth is exactly what it always was.

That is where the textbook lesson ends. What this book wants to carry away from that night is a different lesson, and a more valuable one.

Do the arithmetic. On a single-zero wheel, a specified run of twenty-six blacks has a probability of roughly one in 137 million—no wonder the room was certain it could not continue. But change the scale of the question: how many times does a roulette wheel spin, worldwide, in a year? A one-in-a-million event, across tens of millions of repetitions, is **a scheduled visitor**—the only things you do not know are the date and the address. That night in 1913 was not a miracle. It was an ordinary shift on the roster of the law of large numbers, and it simply happened to be assigned to Monte Carlo. **Rare enough, multiplied by often enough, equals certain.** That is what the twenty-six blacks were actually saying.

Now replace the wheel with your trading system.

* * *

Say your system wins 60% of the time—a genuinely good number. Question: what is the probability of five losses in a row? Taken as one group, 0.4 to the fifth power, about 1%. That sounds safe. But you will not trade five times. You will trade a thousand, and inside that thousand sit **996** overlapping five-trade windows, each one a separate draw. Run it to the end: the probability of at least one five-loss streak in a thousand trades is **over 99%**; at least one seven-loss streak, about six in ten; eight in a row, about a third. Stretch the career to ten thousand trades—a few years' volume for an intraday or short-term trader—and **even the eight-loss streak approaches inevitability.** With enough windows, every small probability reports for duty. Same mathematics as the wheel that night.

And a losing streak is only the skeleton of a drawdown. An equity curve does not need consecutive losses to fall into a deep hole—three losses, a win, four more losses, and the hole goes on being dug. There is a nastier statistical regularity behind that: **the longer the sample, the more likely the known maximum drawdown gets broken.** The deepest hole in your system's history is only the answer it turned in on a finite sample; keep trading, and a longer streak or a crueler ordering of wins and losses will rewrite the record sooner or later. Put another way: **the historical maximum drawdown of any live equity curve is an underestimate of its true maximum drawdown**—the deepest hole is, with high probability, always still ahead of you.

Which brings us back to the ruler this book keeps recalibrating: what is certain and what is not. **A deep drawdown will happen—that is certain**, its probability written into those few lines of multiplication above, and it hears no appeals. **Whether the drawdown leads to zero is not certain**; that depends on the combination of two things—whether your edge is real, and how you bet. The last chapter showed that a fixed fraction can never mathematically reach absolute zero. But if the edge is imaginary, the cost machine (Chapter Four) will grind away your purchasing power, certainly and slowly; a fixed fraction guarantees only that you die slowly, not that you live. Put the two dimensions together and the conclusion is one line. **Time does not kill. Time only magnifies. If the edge is real, time is a friend; if the edge is false, time is an executioner; and either way, the deep hole is on the schedule.**

There is another kind of zero that the math books do not carry, and it arrives far earlier than the mathematical one: **the give-up point.** Sixty percent of the account is left, but ten percent of your confidence is. Or the backer withdraws. Or the conversation at home cannot be won. The overwhelming majority of trading careers do not end at a zero balance; they end when a drawdown touches some psychological or practical limit and the person leaves—and the place where they leave is, more often than not, the bottom of the hole. That line is the one that actually needs budgeting.

* * *

Pushed downward, this certainty yields three corollaries.

First: size your positions for the hole you have not seen yet—not for the average loss, and not for the deepest one on record. The average loss is the normal state, and it is never the normal state that kills; the historical maximum is merely an underestimate, and it earns a place in the denominator of a sizing formula only after you multiply it by a safety factor. This meshes with the last chapter: position size is the one variable you control, and the target it should be aimed at is the drawdown that is certain to arrive and unknown in depth.

Second: a losing streak is not evidence that the system has failed—unless it exceeds a budget you calculated in advance. This is the corollary in this chapter that saves money on the spot. Before you trade at all, use your win rate to work out how many five-loss and seven-loss streaks your system should produce over the next thousand trades, and write those numbers into a sheet of expected behavior. Then, when the streak arrives, your task is not to review every trade hunting for what went wrong—**inside the budget, the answer is that nothing went wrong; the system is breathing normally**—your task is to check one thing: is it inside the budget? The way most people kill a profitable system is exactly this. In the middle of a statistically unremarkable losing streak they decide the system is broken, and then they change parameters, switch methods, take revenge on the market—kicking away the ladder at the bottom of the hole. Inside the budget, do not move a muscle. Outside it, halt and investigate. Two settings only, nothing in between.

Third: on a calm day, define your give-up point in writing. Where the freeze line sits, how long you stop for once it is touched, what conditions thaw you out—all of it has to be on paper before the drawdown arrives, and for the same reason as in the last chapter: **the value of a rule is that it was signed before the impulse.** The bottom of the hole is not a place for making decisions. It is a place for executing decisions already made.

The wheel did not malfunction that night in 1913. It was doing a wheel's job, honoring probability one spin at a time, indifferent to the convictions of the crowd around it. The week your equity curve falls into a deep hole is usually the same: it is not sounding an alarm, it is breathing on schedule. **The real question was never whether the hole comes—this chapter has nailed that answer down—but whether, on the day it comes, your size, your budget, and your line were written down long before.**

(End of Chapter Eleven)

Chapter Twelve

Fifty Bankers

Certainty 12: The margin arithmetic is certain—at leverage L, an adverse move of 1/L puts you out.

March 8, 2022. Early morning, London time.

The paper loss on Xiang Guangda's short nickel position, by market and press estimates at the time, was already on the order of **ten billion dollars**.

His silhouette appeared in Chapter Nine; now bring him to the front of the stage. China's commodity world calls him Big Shot—founder of Tsingshan Holding Group, the largest producer of nickel and stainless steel on earth. On the London Metal Exchange he had accumulated short positions of more than 150,000 tonnes of nickel, roughly five times the LME's entire inventory and an eighth of open interest. This was no gambler's naked short. He owned real mountains of nickel, he owned the whole supply chain, and he understood the metal better than almost anyone alive. He judged that nickel would fall—and, **spoiler, he judged correctly**.

But between March 4 and March 8, the squeeze the war in Ukraine had lit took nickel from about $29,000 straight through $100,000: more than triple, in three sessions. Every dollar of increase worsened the book on 150,000 tonnes by $150,000. The margin calls came in like a rising tide, each wave higher than the last, and his brokers back home had already begun force-liquidating part of the position—**and the buying that forced liquidation generated pushed the price higher still, triggering larger calls.** That afternoon, with the paper loss above ten billion, it was not only Tsingshan hanging by a thread: several brokers had been dragged to the edge of insolvency, and the survival of the LME itself was in question.

Within hours, **more than fifty bankers** had arrived at his office to wait for a plan. He said one thing: "We are confident we can get through this."

Then came a rescue that appears in no textbook. A bank syndicate led by JPMorgan signed a standstill agreement—**margin calls suspended, and a commitment not to liquidate his positions**. The LME canceled eight hours of trading and shut the market for a week, which was the subject of Chapter Nine. Chinese banks pushed in credit. Four months later nickel fell back, exactly as he had said it would; he unwound the shorts at his leisure for a total loss of about a billion dollars—on Tsingshan's scale, a shallow scar. Big Shot walked away whole, and the company went on expanding.

Now read the story backwards: **a man whose call on direction was completely correct needed a syndicate's waiver, an exchange's change of rules, and fifty bankers pulling an all-nighter in order to live until the day the call paid off.** His judgment did not save him. Three other things did—and of those three, you have none.

* * *

THE CERTAINTY OF THIS CHAPTER IS THE THING THAT WAS HUNTING him that afternoon. It fits on one line.

At leverage L, an adverse move of 1/L takes your capital to zero. Ten times leverage: 10% against you and you are cleaned out. Fifty times: 2%. And at the five hundred times the retail foreign exchange industry hands out so generously, **0.2%**—less than EUR/USD breathes on an ordinary trading day. That is only the theoretical terminus, besides: the maintenance margin call line is drawn short of zero, so the actual death comes earlier.

What most needs seeing in that formula is the variables it **does not contain**. There is no term for whether your judgment is correct, none for where the price eventually goes, none for "three more months and it would have been proved." **A margin system does not evaluate opinions. It audits paths**: every stretch of road every candle has traveled since you opened, settled in full, in real time. Xiang Guangda's eventual correctness does not exist inside the formula—the formula recognizes only the price on the screen at that instant. Right or wrong on direction decides whether you deserve to win. Path multiplied by leverage decides whether you live to. **The market can tolerate your being wrong, as long as you are small. The market can kill your being right, as long as you are big.**

Which exposes what leverage actually is. It is sold to you as a multiplier on returns. Its real function is **an error quota**: leverage does not determine how fast you can make money, it determines how many times you can be wrong, how deeply, and for how long. For the lightly levered, a mistaken call is a scratch on the account, with a next one behind it and ten after that. For the heavily levered, the quota covers one ordinary fluctuation—he is not trading a view, he is praying for a path. The same candle is data to the first man and a verdict to the second.

There is one more layer, written for the market as a whole. **Margin arithmetic does not merely liquidate individuals. It is the fuel of extreme moves.** Replay those three days in nickel: price rises, calls trigger, forced buying, price rises again, larger calls—Xiang Guangda's own brokers, liquidating his position, tightened the noose another turn with their own hands. That unreasonable vertical line you see on a chart usually does not have opinions trading underneath it. **It has arithmetic liquidating.** A chain of other people's 1/L thresholds tripping in sequence, each corpse the fuel for the next leg. Once you see this, an extreme move stops being madness and becomes machinery: the market has not lost its reason, the margin formula is executing in bulk.

* * *

PUSHED DOWNWARD, THIS CERTAINTY YIELDS THREE COROLLARIES.

First: measure leverage in volatility, never in nerve. Before opening, answer two questions. How much does this instrument breathe on a normal trading day? How many such breathing days does my leverage accommodate? The liquidation price and the margin call price are two specific numbers; **compute them and write them down before you click.** Knowing your own price of death is part of the qualification to open a position at all. Anything that needs the market to refrain from normal fluctuation in order to survive is not a position. It is a will.

Second: translate leverage into an error budget, then set it against your holding period. The longer the hold, the wilder the path—a trend position must survive more pullbacks, more chop, more false breakouts, which demands more tolerance of path, which forces the leverage ceiling down. A short period with a tight stop can carry relatively high leverage; a long period with a wide path must carry low leverage. **A mismatch between leverage and holding period is the standard recipe for the death called "right on direction, wiped out anyway"**—Xiang Guangda's ten-billion-dollar fright was, at bottom, an industrial-cycle judgment settled on a futures-cycle path.

Third: you do not have fifty bankers—so the only standstill agreement available to you is one you sign with yourself, in advance. Big Shot survived the tide of margin calls on waivers negotiated after the crisis arrived. You cannot negotiate a waiver. But you can write one before the crisis comes: **low leverage is the retail version of a bank syndicate.** It grants you, ahead of time, an exemption from margin calls along the extreme path, and lets you cross without anyone's mercy. This is the third appearance of the same sentence in this book, and it will appear again: the value of a rule is that it was signed before you needed it.

That afternoon, fifty bankers crowded into an office to hear one man say, "We are confident we can get through this." He did get through it—on judgment, and on ten billion dollars' worth of forbearance. The margin formula took no part in any of the negotiations. Every second, it multiplied price by position, subtracted equity, produced a number, and looked at that number to see whether it was enough to keep you at the table. **It doesn't hate you. It doesn't help you. It is simply never late.**

(End of Chapter Twelve)

Chapter Thirteen

The Shake Tax

Certainty 13: Compounding is asymmetric—a 50% loss takes a 100% gain to undo; volatility is itself a cost.

On November 6, 2008, a pair of twin funds was born on the same day.

One was called FAS, three times long US financial stocks: for every 1% the financial index rose, it rose 3%. The other was FAZ, three times short: for every 1% the index fell, it rose 3%. A perfect mirror—logically, whether financials went up or down, one of the brothers had to make a killing, and together they should roughly wash. With the crisis at full boil, FAZ ripped higher, several times over in a matter of weeks, the toast of the market.

Three years later, in the autumn of 2011, look at the report card. The underlying financial index had been through the collapse and the recovery, a long round trip back to near where it started—directionally, three years of marking time. And the mirror twins? **FAS, the long, was down about 85%. FAZ, the short, was down about 99%.**

Two funds that were exact mirrors of one another, both close to annihilation, over three years in which the underlying barely moved. No fraud, no misappropriation, and the management fee was a rounding error—they died of a cost that issues no invoice. To see the killer, go back to grade school and do three sums.

* * *

Sum one: asymmetry. Lose 10% and you need 11.1% to get back. Lose 20%, you need 25%. Lose 50%, you need 100%. Lose 90%, you need **900%**. There is no psychology in that string of numbers, only arithmetic: the loss is measured against the capital you had before it, the recovery against the stub you have after—**the way down and the way back are not the same road**. The deeper the hole, the steeper the climb, and the steepening accelerates: from -10% to -20%, the repair bill goes from 11% to 25%; from -50% to -60%, it jumps from 100% to 150%. The abyss has a geometry, and the shape is a horn that flares wider the further down you go.

Sum two: the drag that does not care about order. Start with 100. Gain 50%, then lose 50%: 100 → 150 → 75. Reverse it, lose first and then gain: 100 → 50 → 75. Different roads, same destination—75 either way. Up 50 and down 50, an average return of zero, and a quarter of the money is gone. Where did the 25 go? Ground off by the shaking itself. As long as returns fluctuate, the multiplication of compounding must drag the endpoint below the average, and the wider the swings the harder the drag—mathematically, **long-run compound return ≈ mean return minus half the variance** (what finance calls volatility drag). Variance holds exactly the same office in that formula as the spread in Chapter Four and tax in Chapter Six: a fee deducted automatically, by rule. With one difference. **The spread comes with a bill and tax comes with a return to file, but this**

money appears on no statement anywhere—it is the only certain cost in the whole market that does not even print a receipt.

Sum three: the twins' autopsy. The index goes 100 to 120 and back to 100—an unremarkable round trip. FAS, three times long: on day one it gains 60%, to 160; on day two the index falls 16.7%, so it falls 50%, **from 160 to 80**. FAZ, three times short: down 60% to 40 on the first day, up 50% on the second, **to 60**. The index is untouched; one twin is down 20%, the other down 40%—from a single round trip. The years around the financial crisis happened to be the most violent stretch in market history, and round trips like that ran every week. Triple leverage multiplies the daily move by three, and variance goes as the square: **the shake tax rate is multiplied ninefold.** Grind through three years and hundreds of round trips, and the directional gains and losses cancel while the shaking bill is collected in full, every time—and so both sides of the bet died. The twins are the cleanest controlled experiment the financial markets have ever run: **zero out the effect of direction entirely, and exhibit the toxicity of volatility on its own.**

Incidentally, this settles the half-sentences the last two chapters left owing. Chapter Twelve called leverage an error quota—here is its other cost: even if the margin call never comes, leverage multiplies variance, and variance is deducted straight out of compound return. **Leverage charges interest on itself, and the rate is the shaking.** Chapter Six called tax a second levy on volatility—here is the first levy arriving: volatility is collected once through the multiplication of compounding, then again through the asymmetry of the tax code. **One variance, two tollbooths.**

* * *

PUSH THIS CERTAINTY DOWNWARD AND YOU GET THREE COROLLARIES.

One: judge any system by its geometric return, never by its arithmetic mean. "An average annual return of 20%" is a sentence with no content unless the volatility is reported alongside it. A smooth 20% and a wild 20% are two different worlds ten years out—an account taking a steady 10% a year compounds to 1.21 over two years; an account doing +40% and then -20%, the same 10% average, compounds to 1.12. Read the denominator first: maximum drawdown, the size of the swings. Only then the return itself. **Anyone can inflate a numerator. Denominators never lie.**

Two: suppressing volatility is the only improvement on the return side with an arithmetic guarantee. The constitution of this book is that there are no certainties on the return side, and this is the closest thing to an exception: what lower variance adds to compound return requires no forecasting ability, depends on no cooperation from the market, and is paid out directly by the formula. Cut leverage, diversify for real, stay off the wildest stretches of the curve—the accident calendar of Chapter One, drawing its second paycheck here. Every bit of variance you squeeze out lifts the geometric return by half as much, automatically. **Everyone hunts for certainty on the return side and comes back empty. It was there the whole time, standing on the variance side.**

Three: the arithmetic of getting back decides where the freeze line goes. Chapter Eleven said to write down your point of surrender while you are calm; this chapter supplies the mathematical case for where to site it. That horn of recovery is still gentle around -10% (+11% and you are home), begins to steepen at -30% (+43%), and past -50% it is close to sheer. The freeze line exists to **keep the account permanently inside the narrow end of the horn**—it is not emotional comfort, it is denying the situation "I need to double to get home" any chance to occur at all. Stopping at the line is not conceding. It is refusing to walk into the part of the road that keeps getting steeper.

The twins are still listed today, stitching a net asset value that keeps falling toward zero back together with one reverse split after another, still on offer to anyone who wants a short-term charge—and the prospectus is now covered in warnings that they are not to be held for more than a single day. They taught the whole market a lesson with their own corpses, and the lesson fits on one line: **the market does not even need to know which side you bet. As long as you are shaking, it is charging.**

(End of Chapter Thirteen)

Chapter Fourteen

The Deepest Ocean

Certainty 14: Liquidity is thinnest at the moment you need it most.

In March 2020 the pandemic detonated the world's markets. US equities tripped the circuit breaker four times in ten days—everybody remembers that part. But the thing that put the chill down the spines of central bankers was not the stock market. It was a much quieter corner.

The US Treasury market, twenty trillion dollars in scale, the bedrock of the global financial system: bank regulators class it as the equivalent of cash, lenders everywhere on earth take it as collateral, and the price of every risk asset starts from it. The textbook is unambiguous. Crisis comes, money runs to Treasuries, prices rise, yields fall—a century of it, and that is what the words "safe haven" literally mean.

Between March 9 and March 18, the textbook was torn up. **While the equity market tripped breaker after breaker, the ten-year Treasury yield rose instead of falling—up roughly 65 basis points in seven trading days.** Meaning that at the peak of the panic, the safest asset on earth was being dumped, and **there were not enough buyers to be found**. Bid-ask spreads and market impact costs blew out to their worst since the 2008 crisis. Order book depth bottomed on March 12 and 13. Off-the-run issues—Treasuries that are not from the most recent auction—went briefly close to unquoted. The basis between cash and futures cracked open and the arbitrage relationships stopped working. **Even the "risk-free" market itself had begun to come apart.**

Who was selling? The central bank studies afterwards produced the roster. Foreign official institutions, dumping Treasuries for dollars to defend their own currencies. Mutual funds, selling into a wave of redemptions. Heavily leveraged hedge funds, selling to meet margin calls—the forced-liquidation machine of Chapter Twelve, running at full speed inside the deepest market humans have. A long roster, every motive different, all of them doing exactly one thing: **they were not selling what they wanted to sell, they were selling what could be sold.** In a crisis, nobody dumps the assets on their book that nobody wanted in the first place—every demand for cash converges, with no coordination at all, on the deepest pool in the market. And so the deepest pool takes the most concentrated pumping.

And the other side? Three-quarters of Treasury trading passes across dealer balance sheets, and the dealers' sheets were already full from absorbing the selling of the previous weeks. On March 12 the Fed opened an emergency repo facility of **$1.5 trillion**—and takers were few. Not for want of money: nobody wanted to expand a balance sheet further. That left one road. The central bank buys the paper itself. On March 15 it announced $700 billion of purchases. On March 23 it dropped the number altogether and switched to buying "**in the amounts needed**." Over the following two weeks the Fed bought an average of **$72 billion** of Treasuries a day, more than a trillion in a quarter, and hauled two-sided quoting back out of the abyss with a printing press.

Hold on to that image: **the deepest ocean on earth, dry enough that somebody had to print seawater.**

* * *

Now the law can be nailed down, and nailed down at the level of mechanism, so that it does not sound like a grievance.

Why does liquidity disappear exactly when you need it? Because **"when you need it most" and "when everyone needs it most" are the same moment**. The reason you need cash—panic, margin calls, redemptions—is the reason everyone else needs cash, and every seller raising cash is simultaneously a liquidity provider walking away. In calm weather, market makers, arbitrageurs and dip buyers stack up layer on layer, and the depth is as thick as an ocean. When the storm comes, the seawater has its own life to save. **The people who supply liquidity are volunteers, never a garrison.** The market makers pulling quotes in Chapter Two, the order-book vacuum in Chapter Eight—that is the same body of volunteers exercising the same freedom. Peak demand and trough supply do not collide by bad luck. They are **two faces of one coin**, structurally simultaneous.

From which comes this certainty's most insidious corollary: **every liquidity measurement you can take is a reading from a time when you did not need it.** The everyday spread, the everyday depth, the everyday slippage—the numbers are real, and they describe a market you will not be using. It is a fire policy that voids itself on the day of the fire: the wording is elegant, the claims line is open, and at the moment the building catches, the insurer is running down the stairs beside you.

Turn back through the earlier chapters and four accidents turn out to be four faces of one law. The yen flash crash (Chapter One) was a **vacuum of the clock**—a no-man's-land written into the calendar. The Swiss franc (Chapter Two) was a **vacuum of event**—the market makers leaving the room ahead of a policy bomb. The flash crash (Chapter Eight) was a **vacuum of speed**—machines pulling quotes faster than a human blink. March 2020 was a **vacuum of system**—the whole market raising cash at once, with not enough ocean to go round. Different triggers, identical ending: **at the exact moment you need the order book thick, one side of it empties.**

* * *

PUSH THIS CERTAINTY DOWNWARD AND YOU GET THREE COROLLARIES.

One: the slippage in a stress test must be a tail value, never a mean. Mean slippage is the price of a postage stamp in peacetime, and a stress test is a test of wartime. Put your system's exit cost in at five to ten times the everyday figure and see whether it dies—**if it dies under that assumption, it is already dead now, and the market simply has not got round to telling you.** Chapter Two said a stop's fill price is uncertain. This chapter supplies the quantitative floor: the uncertainty always points toward the more expensive side.

Two: the ceiling on a position is set by the day the door is narrowest, not by the average width of the door. The real size of a position is not the fraction of your account it occupies, it is the fraction it occupies of the exit on a vacuum day. Normal depth swallowing ten times your position does not make you safe. The door you have to get through is the door on the day everybody is pushing at it. Anyone holding a large position in a shallow market is holding paper wealth: **on the statement it is worth that much, provided you never need to turn it into money.**

Three: the only countercyclical liquidity is the liquidity you brought yourself. Market liquidity is procyclical everywhere: abundant in peace, evaporated in war. One thing only runs the other way—the cash in your hand, the margin you have not used, the leverage you kept down. In calm weather it looks idle, a loss of efficiency; on the day everyone else is forced to sell, **not being forced is the largest edge on the floor**. That day you can even turn around and be the scarce buyer, collecting other people's have-tos. (The complete version of that business is half told in the food-chain chapters ahead, and the last chapter comes back to it.) Carry your own fire and you do not need an insurer.

The March 2020 story has an ending that belongs to central banks alone: the Fed can print the ocean back. **You cannot.** So your whole apparatus—slippage assumptions, position ceilings, leverage, cash—has to be built on a single premise: **that day, nobody comes to save you.** The good news is that a system designed on that premise does not need saving.

(End of Chapter Fourteen)

Chapter Fifteen

The Only Thing That Rose That Day

Certainty 15: In a crisis, correlations converge on 1.

Friday, August 21, 1998.

In the morning session a merger arbitrage trade went wrong—the target's share price halved, and Long-Term Capital Management lost $160 million on that one deal. An isolated event, ordinary risk in the arbitrage business. Then a position in US bonds lost $100 million. Then another $100 million went in the UK. Then Europe, then swap spreads, then equity index volatility—**table after unrelated table catching fire, one after another, on the same day**. By the close, the day's loss stood at $553 million.

The fund's risk model had done the arithmetic: the worst single-day loss was about $35 million. The real number was **fifteen times** the model's ceiling. That August came to be called a ten-sigma event—work back from the normal distribution the model implied and something like it happens on average once every 3.3×10^{20} years, far longer than the age of the universe. That astronomical figure comes from the post-mortems, not from any report the model itself printed. **A model never gives notice of its own failure.** Someone later supplied the textbook reply: when your ruler produces an impossible reading, the thing to doubt is not reality. **It is the ruler.**

The ruler had a distinguished pedigree. LTCM was founded by John Meriwether, the legendary head of bond trading at Salomon Brothers, and the partner list seated two Nobel laureates in economics—the authors of the option pricing formula themselves. Victor Haghani, the man from Chapter Ten who would one day hand out $25 apiece and a rigged coin, was among the founding partners. And the fund's central article of faith was, precisely, **diversification**: more than a hundred convergence trades laid across the globe—US swap spreads, European sovereigns, British gilts, the Japanese bond market, merger arbitrage, equity index volatility—positions the historical record showed, over and over, to be almost uncorrelated with one another. Because the book was so diversified, the model judged it extremely safe; because it was safe, 25x leverage looked reasonable; because of the leverage, the notional on their swap book reached $1.25 trillion at one point, 5% of the global market. **Diversification was the foundation of the building. Every floor was built on the phrase "the correlations are low."**

On August 17, Russia devalued the ruble and defaulted on its debt. LTCM's direct exposure to Russia was not large—by the logic of diversification this was supposed to be somebody else's disaster. But over the following weeks **nearly every trade turned against them at once**: every spread in the world that was meant to converge widened together, and every historically unrelated position went down holding hands. In August alone the fund lost 44%. Equity fell from more than four billion dollars before the crisis toward a few hundred million, while a hundred billion of assets still sat on the book—**nobody added**

leverage; it inflated on its own, from 25x to more than 100x (the arithmetic of Chapter Twelve: shrink the denominator and the multiple flies up by itself). On September 23 the New York Fed sat fourteen banks around one table and assembled $3.6 billion in exchange for 90% of the fund. Not charity. Too much would have been crushed if that body fell.

The epitaph is the coldest part of the story. Over the next year or two those spreads **converged, almost every one of them, exactly as predicted**. Trade by trade, the judgments were basically right. The nickel drama of an earlier chapter had already had its premiere here—**right, and dead**. They simply could not survive, as one firm, to the day of payment.

* * *

There is only one question. A hundred trades, historically uncorrelated: why did they go to their deaths hand in hand in the same month?

Because the correlation matrix measured the wrong object. **Correlation in calm periods measures the relationship between assets and assets; what operates in a crisis is the relationship between holders and holders.** LTCM's hundred trades were spread over five continents and a dozen asset classes, and they shared one thing that appeared nowhere in the matrix: **the same kind of people held them.** Bank proprietary desks and arbitrage funds all over the world carried convergence positions much like LTCM's. Russia went off, and everybody took margin calls at the same time, cut risk at the same time, sold whatever could be sold at the same time—so Japanese bonds, British spreads and American merger arb were knocked down together by a single wave of deleveraging. On the surface, a hundred trades. Underneath, **one trade: short panic, long calm**—signed with a hundred different names.

Dig one layer deeper and you reach the bedrock of this certainty: **money is the only common factor every asset has.** The definition of a crisis is that everyone needs the same thing at the same instant, and the thing is cash. To raise it, people sell everything that can be sold: stocks, bonds, gold, bitcoin. In that week of March 2020 in the last chapter, gold fell alongside Treasuries and equities and the entire safe-haven category failed at once—gold had not betrayed the haven; **the people holding gold needed dollars**. In normal times, assets each have their own story and go their own way. In a crisis every story collapses into one question: can this be turned into money right now? And then everything moves in one direction. The old line traders pass around is the best folk version of this certainty: **on the day of a crash, the only thing that goes up is correlation.**

* * *

PUSH THIS CERTAINTY DOWNWARD AND YOU GET THREE COROLLARIES.

One: audit diversification by common factor, not by instrument count. Ask every position in the book the same question: **when the crisis comes, who is forced to sell this?** Positions with the same answer are one position, however far apart the tickers. Eight different currency pairs, if all eight rise and fall with a single global risk-appetite switch, are not eight-fold diversification; they are one position signed eight times. Real diversification diversifies the sources of have-to—different forced sellers, different liquidation mechanisms, different funding chains. Diversification by counting ticker symbols holds only in calm markets, and calm markets never needed it.

Two: in a stress test, set the portfolio's correlation to 1 outright. Correlations measured in calm are fit only for calm—this is the twin clause of Chapter Eight's rule that a conclusion is bound to a data version: correlation is bound to a market state. To stress the book, assume every position runs the same way on the same day and the hedging side fails entirely, then see whether the account dies; derive the total position ceiling backward from that everything-one-way scenario. This is not pessimism. It is building on bedrock instead of sand—and sand is very firm most of the time.

Three: inside your portfolio sits somebody else's portfolio. What beat LTCM's hundred trades was not their instruments; it was that other people held the same positions. Which makes **crowding a risk parameter**, on the same footing as volatility: the more universally admired a trade is, the more it is the market's consensus position, the harder it falls in a crisis—because the queue at the door is longest (the narrow door of Chapter Fourteen, now with a line outside it). Ask yourself regularly: how much of what I hold is the entire market's default answer right now? The higher that fraction, the lower the grade of your "diversification."

The lesson usually drawn from that fund is the danger of leverage, or the arrogance of models. Both are true, and neither is the bottom layer. The bottom layer is this: **diversification can protect you from an accident in any one asset, and nothing can protect you from everyone needing money at once.** On the day of the crisis, your portfolio holds two kinds of asset: money, and things that need to become money.

(End of Chapter Fifteen)

Chapter Sixteen

The Plane No One Man Can Fly

Certainty 16: Your execution discipline is the least certain component in the entire system—and that fact itself is certain.

October 30, 1935. Wright Field, Ohio.

On the runway stood the largest land-based aircraft humanity had ever built: the Boeing Model 299, four engines, machine guns pointing in every direction, and a nickname coined by a reporter that would ring through the Second World War—the Flying Fortress. This was the acceptance flight of the Army's competition, and Boeing had staked everything on it. The outcome was hardly in doubt. The 299 crushed its rivals on range, speed and bomb load, and the Army was already planning an initial order of sixty-five.

The cockpit held the best men available too. The pilot was Major Ployer P. Hill, chief of the flying branch at Wright Field, one of the most experienced test pilots in the service; also aboard was Boeing's chief test pilot, Les Tower—the man who had flown this aircraft into existence.

That morning the 299 roared into the air, climbed to about three hundred feet, stalled, hit the ground, and burned. Hill and Tower died of their injuries.

The finding of the investigation made the whole industry catch its breath. The aircraft was **faultless**—structure, engines, controls, aerodynamics, all sound. The cause was one lever: the gust lock, which holds the control surfaces still on the ground so that a high wind cannot damage them, had not been released before takeoff. Tower realized it in the air, but from where he sat he could not reach the lock. The finest pilot in the service, killed by forgetting a single action.

The newspapers' verdict survives to this day: **this plane is too complicated for one man to fly.** Boeing lost the competition.

And then history came to a fork. Faced with the fact that even the best pilot forgets things, there are two conventional replies. Find better pilots—but Hill was already the best. Train harder—but forgetting is not a deficit of skill and cannot be drilled away. The pilots at Wright Field took a third road, one you can only walk after swallowing your pride: **admit that the problem is not the complexity of the aircraft but the capacity of human memory—and then write a list.** Check it item by item before takeoff, check it in the air, check it before landing. That simple. Simple to the point of humiliation: the elite of the air corps would henceforth take off reading off a piece of paper.

The result: the first twelve aircraft of the type flew, with the checklist aboard, **1.8 million miles without an accident**. The plane no one man could fly went into production as the B-17, more than twelve thousand seven hundred of them built, and became the backbone of the Allied bombing campaign. The checklist was written from then on into the law of military and civil aviation worldwide. **Not one rivet on the aircraft was changed, and no human being grew a better memory. One**

thing changed, and one only: nobody ever again took off on memory.

* * *

Now move the story across to your own desk.

Your system has a 299 of its own: the backtest. Every backtest report seats a perfect pilot in the cockpit—**every signal taken 100% of the time, the stop never moved, the size always compliant, the eleventh trade after ten losses no different from the first**. The live cockpit seats a human: after three losses, "I'll skip this one"; on an open profit, "hold it a while longer"; just before the stop is swept, "move it out a touch, only this once"; and once the losses have gone numb, double up. The largest source of divergence between backtest and live account has never been slippage, and never the spread. **It is the operator.**

And the human error rate is not even a constant. It has one utterly vicious property: **it moves with pressure.** In quiet markets you really are a model of discipline. On the sixth consecutive loss, with a fortune in front of you, with panic filling the screen—precisely when the system most needs reliability, your reliability slides toward its floor. Sound familiar? Chapter Fourteen, just now: liquidity is thinnest at the moment you need it most. **Your discipline is the liquidity inside your own account**—plentiful enough in quiet times to make you confident, and pulling its quotes alongside the market makers when the crisis comes.

Take inventory of the fifteen components covered so far. The spread is measurable. Slippage can be given a tail value. Swap is written in the fine print. Margin is arithmetic. Correlation can be stress-tested. Every one of those parts has a failure mode that can be modeled. One part cannot: **the operator.** The sixty-one people in Chapter Ten already ran the experiment for you —a 60% edge face-up, posted on the wall in black and white, and three in ten went bust. That is this component's failure rate as measured in a laboratory. Which makes this chapter's certainty stand, and with a certain paradoxical beauty: the only certain thing about you is your uncertainty; and the question of which component in the whole system is the least reliable has an answer that is **one hundred percent reliable**.

This is the first-principles case for automation, and note that it is not the case usually advertised. **It is not that the machine is smarter**—the code executes the rules you wrote, not one line more, not an ounce of extra wisdom. **It is that the machine's hand does not shake on the sixth losing trade.** Automation is the checklist in its finished form: the checklist lifts compliance from "depends how you feel" to nearly perfect, and the code takes it to 100%. With execution error abolished, the walk-forward validation of Chapter Eight is finally testing the strategy itself and not your last three months of mood.

But be honest all the way down. Automation does not abolish the discipline problem. **It only concentrates discipline into a single button.** However loyal the machine, the switch is still in your hand—on the sixth losing trade, the shaking hand only changes form, from firing off wild orders to switching the thing off. So the final form of discipline is a set of intervention rules: the conditions under which a human may touch the machine—drawdown beyond the budget of Chapter Eleven, or a technical fault, those two and nothing else—and otherwise, **hands off the keyboard**. All of your free will is exercised in the legislature. None of it during execution.

* * *

PUSH THIS CERTAINTY DOWNWARD AND YOU GET THREE COROLLARIES.

One: design yourself as a component; do not train yourself as a hero. Major Hill has already run the hero route on everyone's behalf. Every decision that can be written as a rule before the open—entry conditions, the sizing formula, where the stop goes, the days you do not trade—leave not one of them to the version of you that exists during the session. And begin the checklist at the stupidest end: the first entries on the B-17 list were stupid enough to be a joke, "unlock the control surfaces"—**but what kills you is never the difficult mistake, it is the stupid one**, because difficult mistakes you guard against and stupid ones you think beneath you.

Two: automate in order of emotional pressure × repetition. You do not have to go fully automatic in one step. Start with the links that are clearly ruled, mechanically repetitive, and happen to be executed under maximum pressure: the stop submitted with the order rather than "by hand, when the time comes"; the size produced by a formula rather than "this one feels safe"; the accident calendar applied automatically, the homework of Chapter One. Every link you automate strips one stretch of human improvisation-under-pressure out of the system.

Three: keep an execution log, and audit human intervention as though it were a strategy. Every deviation from the system—the signal skipped, the exit taken early, the stop that got moved—write it down, and settle it separately at month end: what would have happened under full compliance, and what was the net contribution of my interference? Let the data answer the question of what these two hands are worth. Most people uncover an embarrassing fact within three months: **you are the worst-performing strategy in your own account.** The embarrassment does not matter. The day you discover it is the day your checklist is born. The pilots at Wright Field started from an embarrassment too.

The major's name was later cut into the gate of an air force base in Utah: Hill Air Force Base. To be remembered for an accident does not sound like an honor—but aviation understands what he actually left behind. **The checklist came from the very best pilots, not because they doubted their skill, but because they had finally become honest about themselves.** To admit that you are the least reliable part in the system is not a disgrace. It is where systems engineering begins.

Part Two closes here. Seven pieces of defensive mathematics, not one of them about where the market is going. They answer a single question: how to stay alive. In the next part we go and look at the other living things in this market—the food chain.

(End of Chapter Sixteen · End of Part Two)

Part Three

The Structure of the Food Chain

Chapter Seventeen

One Thousand Two Hundred Thirty-Seven Wins, One Loss

Certainty 17: On the other side of your trade there is always someone faster than you, richer than you, and better informed than you.

In March 2014, a filing lodged with the US Securities and Exchange Commission frightened the entire market.

The filer was a company most people had never heard of: Virtu Financial, an electronic market maker. Somewhere in the prospectus sat a chart of daily profit and loss, with a caption of studied understatement: from January 1, 2009 through December 31, 2013, across 1,238 trading days, "**we had one losing day**."

Five years. One thousand two hundred thirty-seven days of making money, one day of losing it. A hit rate of 99.92%. The financial press detonated on contact: "The Holy Grail of trading has been found." The ordinary trader's first reaction was almost physiological: **the market is rigged.** That same month *Flash Boys* was published, high-frequency trading was nailed to the public cross, and Virtu's listing had to be postponed—incidentally, when it refiled a year later the record had become 1,485 days, still with the same solitary loss.

Anger is easy. This chapter wants to do something worth more: read that prospectus as a map.

How did Virtu do it? The document is not remotely coy about it: market making. Quoting both sides at once in dozens of countries and hundreds of markets, buying at the bid, selling at the offer, keeping the difference—**it is the holder of the green square from Chapter Four**. It forecasts nothing. It does not guess direction, does not study fundamentals, does not care what the Fed does. Every one of its trades is a coin flip with a sliver of spread attached as rent, and it flips a few million times a day. The arithmetic of Chapter Eleven runs backwards in its hands: the law of large numbers you need a thousand trades to assemble, it finishes before lunch—the win or loss on any single flip is ground into the mean by sheer repetition before noon, and so a "losing day" becomes mathematically close to impossible. **It does not bet well. It has put a casino inside every fill.** Holding all of that up is speed measured in microseconds, quotes counted in the hundreds of millions, and a real-time risk system—armament priced in units of a billion dollars.

Now digest this chapter's certainty: **that company is in the pool on the other side of your trade.** Every time you press the button, the pool your order enters has Virtus swimming in it, and Citadels, and Jane Streets; funds counting oil tankers from satellites, banks employing former central bankers, machines that saw the quote a few microseconds before you did. This is not conspiracy theory. It is arithmetic performed on the participant list: **water worth fishing collects the best-armed hunters**—the physics of profit-seeking from Chapter Three. So "there is always someone faster, richer, better informed" is not a lament, it is a structure. You do not know whether they are your direct counterparty today. You know they are in the pool, and you know they are not vegetarians.

Most people read despair here. Read one layer further—**the same prospectus marks precisely where they win**: the spread, the microsecond, the front of the queue. Walk onto any of those three plots of ground and you are simply handing money over. But there is another side to the map, and almost nobody turns it over: **every weapon is also a shackle on the man holding it.**

Virtu's near-perfect equity curve rests on real-time risk control and going flat by the close—**its model forbids it to hold an opinion**. Make it carry a position through three weeks of trend and the whole machine is scrap on the spot. The players racing for information hold information that decays by the minute; they have to be out before the news is wrung dry, and they cannot hold anything long. The behemoths running a hundred billion leave footprints coming and going—the subject of Chapter Twenty—and the door frame limits every move they make. Speed ends at the closing bell, information ends at the week, size ends at the width of the door: **every king of a dimension is chained to that dimension by his own throne.** Which leaves blank water on the map. Patience measured in weeks. Size too small to leave a mark. The freedom not to play at all. Discipline written as code (Chapter Sixteen). In those dimensions not one of their weapons can be brought to bear—not for want of wanting, but because their structure will not permit it.

* * *

Push this certainty downward and you get three corollaries.

One: before any strategy goes on the table, run a counterparty audit. One question only: whose money is this supposed to take? If the honest answer is "I'll be a little faster," "I'll know first," "I'll get ahead of the earnings print"—you are walking into the home ground of people armed to the teeth. That is not a strategy, it is a donation. Abandon it now. If the answer is "the inertia of big money that cannot turn," "patience in the statistical sense," "somebody else's have-tos"—then we can keep talking. The old question of Chapter Three is promoted here into an admissions test: **a strategy that cannot say whose pocket the money comes out of is assumed to be taking it out of yours.**

Two: forge "small" into a weapon instead of wearing it as a shame. Write out the structural exemptions of small capital and tape the list to the edge of your screen. You have no impact cost—every door is one you can walk in and out of. You have no redemption pressure—nobody can force your chips out of you at the bottom of the hole. You have no daily P&L review—you can let one trade sit quietly through three weeks. You have no mandate obliging you to be invested—sit flat for three months and nobody docks your pay. **Virtu cannot hold overnight. The fund manager cannot sit flat. The sovereign fund cannot turn around. You can do all three.** Your ground is precisely the set of things the other side is unable to do.

Three: tear up the arms-race purchase order. A faster server, a costlier data feed, a news wire a second ahead of the rest—every item drags you further onto somebody else's home ground, and admission there is priced in billions. Every penny you pay is loose change, and every millisecond you buy is still slow. Infrastructure has exactly one standard: adequate and stable. The armament you should actually be buying makes a list absurdly short—**a longer time scale, and harder discipline**. The first is free; the second Chapter Sixteen taught you how to build. And the beauty of it is that your opponents cannot use either one.

The fire *Flash Boys* lit burned for years, and "the market is rigged" is still the most popular explanation going. This book's version is cooler and a great deal more useful: **the market is not rigged to the point where you cannot win—it is merely armed to the point where you cannot win in their dimensions.** One thousand two hundred thirty-seven wins and one loss is not your death sentence. It is a well-labeled chart: here be dragons, sail around them. The first lesson of the food chain is not to get stronger. It is to see who is at the table, and then—take a chair nobody is fighting over. In the chapters that follow we walk this table and look at every seat in turn.

(End of Chapter Seventeen)

Chapter Eighteen

The Syllabus of Fear

Certainty 18: Around major events the spread is certain to widen, and the timing can be known in advance—the spread is the market's breathing; depth is its lung capacity.

On June 23, 2016, at ten o'clock at night London time, the polls closed on Britain's referendum on leaving the European Union.

Sterling stood above 1.50 against the dollar, its high for the year. The last polls leaned to Remain, and the market had voted its expectation in hard cash: a scare, nothing more, business as usual. After midnight the count came out of Sunderland with Leave far above expectation. A London head of trading left a line behind that night that has been quoted ever since: "**Tin hats on—cable is going to get someone killed.**" Over the next few hours sterling staged the largest single-day collapse in thirty years, from 1.50 straight down through 1.33. Textbooks still use that night's intraday chart to explain what a binary event is.

But this chapter is not about that night. It is about **six days earlier**.

On June 17 the Singapore Exchange put out a notice: in view of the volatility the British referendum might produce, it was

raising margin on the relevant contracts—a "precautionary measure." In the same stretch Hong Kong Exchanges and Clearing and Australia's clearing house quietly told dealers that margin might go up, and might be called intraday. Retail brokers around the world began sending mass emails, all of them worded much the same: over the referendum, margin requirements will rise, **spreads will widen significantly**, gaps are possible, please manage your positions in advance. Look further back still and one-month implied volatility on sterling had been climbing for six straight weeks, up to a seven-year high.

Taste the structure in that. **Nobody knew the result of the referendum—and yet the entire risk apparatus of the global market had put "fear" on the calendar a week ahead.** Exchanges take no view. Market makers do not guess winners. They did precisely one thing: circle that night on the calendar, and collectively raise the price of not knowing. Fear was in the papers, with a date on it.

* * *

TO UNDERSTAND THAT, YOU HAVE TO UNDERSTAND WHAT THE spread actually is.

Every two-sided quote a market maker posts is, in essence, **an option handed out free of charge**: the price sits there, and anyone—including anyone better informed than the maker—can take it at will. Ordinarily this is fine; everybody is about equally ignorant. As an event nears, the risk jumps. What if the other side knows the result half a second before I do? What if the market gaps away after I am filled and I am holding a warehouse of inventory with nowhere to hedge it? So the maker has two choices: sell that option dearer—**widen the spread**—or stop selling it altogether—**pull the quotes and leave the floor**. Which means the spread is never a technical parameter. It is **the market's live price on not knowing what happens next**. Narrow, and the people quoting feel solid. Wide, and either somebody knows what you do not, or nobody dares know anything at all.

Which is the metaphor this book now formally adopts: **the spread is the market's breathing; the depth of the book is its lung capacity.** A healthy market breathes long and even. As an event closes in, the breath goes shallow and fast—and it usually does so **before the price moves**. The price is still, and the spread has already widened its eyes, because the makers have begun to turn sideways. To read the breathing is to own a free early-warning instrument. As for the most dangerous moment of all, Chapter Two has already staged it: **the lungs empty first, and the gauge lags behind**—in the instant before the franc came off its peg the spread still looked normal and the depth had already gone. Before breathing stops there is often an unnatural moment of calm.

Now the chapter's certainty can be nailed down exactly. **What cannot be known is the outcome. What is certain to happen, at a time written on the calendar, is the widening of the spread.** Non-farm payrolls, CPI, central bank decisions, referendums—in the seconds to tens of minutes around those moments, widening is not a probability, it is a fixed action written into the risk code of every market maker on earth, kin to the swap calendar of Chapter Five: **fear has a syllabus, and it is published years in advance.** Brexit night merely turned the law into a public lecture. The market may not know the result—but it knows precisely when it will not know.

* * *

Push this certainty downward and you get three corollaries.

One: fold the event calendar into the cost model. The same signal, landing inside a data-release window, can cost five to ten times as much to execute—the green square of Chapter Four puts up a temporary extension at these moments. An expected value computed off a single fixed spread is systematically wrong inside the window. Two fixes, take your pick. Filter at the signal layer: no new positions for N minutes either side of an event, cut the window out of the system entirely. Or bill the cost parameter by time slot, so that signals in event windows carry their real toll. The accident calendar of Chapter One draws its third paycheck here.

Two: put the live spread on your risk dashboard and read it as an instrument rather than swallow it as a cost. Most people feel the spread only at the moment of the fill. The smarter use is to watch it. **An unscheduled widening is itself information**—nothing on the calendar and the breathing suddenly goes short means something you do not know about is happening: stand down first, investigate afterwards. Run it the other way and the spread coming back in after an event is the closing bell on digestion. If you want in, wait for the breathing to settle. The instrument runs around the clock and costs nothing, and almost nobody looks at it.

Three: when the breathing is short, do nothing. The discipline list for event windows is brief and hard. No new positions. Cancel resting orders—including the ones you believe are protecting you, because as Chapter Two showed, a stop that becomes a market order on trigger will, in a vacuum, deliver only the worse of its two promises. For positions already on, pick one of two in advance: a stop wide enough to survive the storm, with size cut to match, or an exit before it starts. It reduces to a single line. **Do not hand your fate, at the moment the market is holding its breath, to a mechanism that needs the market to be breathing normally.**

There is a small loop at the end. Three and a half months after the referendum, in the Asian early morning of October 7, sterling fell almost 9% in forty seconds for no reason at all—most of the press, working from a different quote feed, put it at 6%—attributed afterwards to algorithms and a fat finger, the offense committed in exactly the liquidity-vacuum window of Chapter One: the aftershock of the event picked the thinnest page on the calendar to land on. And the news worth taking away from that June night was never how far sterling fell. **It is that six days earlier, fear had already been in the papers. Anyone who can read a calendar does not need to predict a referendum.**

(End of Chapter Eighteen)

Chapter Nineteen

Don't Mistake Yourself for the Moon

Certainty 19: Small money cannot start a trend, only recognize one and ride it—capital size × rebalancing horizon decides which tier of the market you live on.

Friday, October 21, 2022, the New York session.

USD/JPY had just printed 151.95—**a thirty-two-year high**. It had been one of the smoothest trends of the year: the Fed raising rates toward 4% to crush inflation, the Bank of Japan holding the line at negative rates, the gap between them opening into a wide mouth, the dollar chewing its way up from 115 to 152. Trend funds, macro funds and carry players the world over lay comfortably on the same side, long dollar, short yen. The chart was clean enough to teach from.

Then, with no news and no announcement, USD/JPY **fell vertically** in the space of a few minutes, down almost 4% at the low, straight into 146—over five yen of instantaneous reversal, the largest one-day fall since March 2020. Stops on short-yen positions went off in whole fields. The desks erupted: was that intervention? Tokyo declined to comment. This is what stealth intervention means—act, admit nothing, let the market guess. The guessing is part of the weapon.

The data published later confirmed all of it. That day Japan's Ministry of Finance threw **¥5.62 trillion, about $37 billion**, at the market: the largest single-day currency intervention in history at the time, and with the days that followed, ¥6.35 trillion for October. And this was already the second blow. On September 22 the Ministry had carried out **its first yen-buying intervention since 1998**, roughly $20 billion, knocking the price from 145.9 down toward 141. Two months, ¥9.18 trillion in all, some $60 billion.

Now the chapter's real question: **what did that $60 billion buy?**

The answer sobers anyone who stands in awe of power. **A few weeks.** After September's blow the engine of the rate differential did not so much as shudder; the trend caught its breath, turned back, and a month later printed a higher high—which is what produced October's second blow. The second was bigger, harder and better concealed, and it too only held the price down. It did not bend the direction. The real reversal came in November: US inflation came in below expectations and the market began to price a Fed turn—**the expected rate differential loosened.** USD/JPY fell further in the following days than both interventions combined, and from that point it genuinely turned. The tide went out on its own, and did overnight what $60 billion had not.

* * *

The story lights up the market's tiered structure all at once, and it also lights up the place where that structure usually gets told wrong.

Get the causation straight first. Who starts a trend? Not the trend funds—**CTAs have no view; they obey nobody and they anticipate nothing.** They follow price; price moves and they climb aboard and amplify. The real chain runs: **policy and real-economy flows—the US–Japan rate differential, trade flows, allocation flows—manufacture a price trend → trend funds recognize it and amplify it → smaller players feed in the ripples of the amplified version.** This is a chain of flow, not a chain of command. Nobody takes orders from anybody. A small body of water simply cannot, physically, fight a large one.

One image nails the three tiers: **tide, amplifier, ripple.** Rate differentials and sovereign-scale flows are the tide—measured in months and quarters, in hundreds of billions, deciding which way the sea level tilts. Trend funds are the amplifier—tens of billions, measured in weeks, pulling the tide's direction into that handsome line on the chart. Intraday and short-term players live in the ripples, where every wrinkle between the tides is their entire world. And the yen war of 2022 gave us the rare sight of **both ends of the chain on trial at once**. The Ministry of Finance, seated high above the amplifiers, could slap every CTA on the planet into hunting for its own stops—absolute violence from the tier above onto the tier below. And the Ministry itself, facing the tide of the rate differential, could buy no more than a few weeks with $60 billion. **Not even a sovereign can move the tide. It can only ambush the surfers.**

So which tier are you on? Do the humble arithmetic. Daily turnover in the currency market runs into the trillions of dollars, and starting a genuine trend takes net flow in the tens of billions, sustained over months. Against that scale your order does not amount to a ripple—**you cannot start anything, and this is not a matter of ability, it is arithmetic.** But read the sentence to the end, because the second half is the chapter's real subject: not being able to start one does not stop you riding one. And the rider's entire job is a single task—**decide whether the tide has moved, and whether it is still there.**

* * *

PUSH THIS CERTAINTY DOWNWARD AND YOU GET THREE COROLLARies.

One: always rewrite "I found a trend" as "I recognized somebody else's flow." Each time you see a trend, ask first what its tide is. A rate differential? A policy divergence? An industry-scale reallocation of capital? And is that tide still running? The answer sets the standard by which you judge the trend alive or dead: **a violent counter-move while the tide is unchanged is an ambush, not a reversal**—the trend making new highs after the September intervention is the textbook demonstration. When the tide genuinely loosens, as it did on November's inflation print, the trend dies by itself with nobody intervening at all. To judge a trend, look at the engine of the tide, not at the violence of a single day.

Two: even a position with the big trend must be built to take a sovereign-grade slap at any moment. The people lying on the correct side on October 21 were swept out anyway by five yen of instant reversal—right direction, no exemption from the path, the old account from Chapter Twelve. Players several tiers above you have the power to manufacture an instant reversal at whatever moment they choose, and they prefer to do it when you are most crowded and most comfortable (Chapter Fifteen: the most crowded trade takes the worst beating). So: a currency with a clear propensity for intervention is itself a position parameter, and stop distance and leverage have to leave room for one slap that changes nothing about the tide and is more than enough to clear the floor.

Three: recognize the one dividend of your own tier—turning around costs you nothing. The tide layer rebalances on a quarterly clock; the amplifiers have to grind back over their own footprints to turn, the subject of the next chapter. **In the whole chain only you, the smallest, can turn without disturbing anyone, boarding and stepping off at zero impact cost.** The dividend comes with one condition: do not mismatch. Run a sovereign fund's holding period on a retail account's capital and your account dies before the tide finishes running. Chase a tide at intraday frequency and costs (Chapter Four) eat your patience. Your capital size × your reaction speed decides which tier you ought to be living on—live on the right one and the hierarchy is not oppression, it is division of labour.

The role the Ministry's $60 billion finally took in history was to give the whole world a free lesson in hierarchy: **it won every battle and lost to the tide**—and when the tide turned, it turned without a shot fired. A trend never belongs to the people who follow it, and never to the people who ambush it. It belongs to the people who manufacture the flow. Your entire job is to work out which way the water is going, and then ride it. **Don't mistake yourself for the moon.**

(End of Chapter Nineteen)

Chapter Twenty

The Waterline

Certainty 20: Big money going in and out is certain to leave traces—slicing can hide the rhythm, but not the net direction.

In early 2012 an unsolved case was going around the credit derivatives market.

An index called CDX IG9—a bundle of credit default swaps on more than a hundred investment-grade companies—was doing something that made no sense. **The price of the index kept coming in below the sum of all its components.** By the logic of arbitrage a gap like that should be erased on the instant, the old law of Chapter Three. Instead of converging it kept stretching wider, as though an invisible hand were leaning on the index and selling, one side only, day after day.

London's trading floors already had a name for it. One hedge fund manager recalled later: "Whenever there was a big move in the CDS market, you knew—**it was the whale.**" Nobody had seen the whale, nobody knew who it was or who it worked for; and yet everybody was certain there was something enormous underwater, because **the waterline does not lie**. That spread which refused to converge was the shadow the creature's bulk cast onto prices. In February 2012 Boaz Weinstein of Saba Capital recommended the trade publicly at an investment conference—buy the abnormally cheap IG9. He did not know the whale's name. He only needed to know this: bend a price into that shape and there is mass underwater, and something that big has to move eventually. The hedge funds heard and came swarming, and took up position, collectively, on the far side of the whale.

The whale's identity, when it surfaced a few months later, stunned the world: **JPMorgan's own Chief Investment Office** —the bank universally credited with the sharpest risk management in the business, whose trader Bruno Iksil had sold tens of billions of dollars of protection on IG9. What came next was more astonishing still. The position was too large to leave—**any reduction would drive the price into its own face**. So the whale chose the other road: defend the position. Keep buying, hold the price up with new positions, do not let the loss develop. In a single quarter the notional size of the book swelled by nearly three times, past $150 billion. **Everything done to hide the footprints left bigger footprints.** The higher the waterline was propped, the more hunters gathered on the other side.

In April the press exposed the "London Whale," and Jamie Dimon waved it away: a tempest in a teapot. On May 10 the bank admitted a $2 billion loss and the stock fell 11% in two days. By year end the loss had settled at **$6.2 billion**. Dimon later said one thing at the Senate hearing: "I was dead wrong." More than a billion in fines, executives gone, a three-hundred-page Senate report for posterity—and, with some irony, JPMorgan still booked a record $21.3 billion of profit that year. The whale's death was a scar on the bank. **On the market, it was a public lecture.**

* * *

THE CONTENT OF THAT LECTURE IS THIS CHAPTER'S CERTAINTY, AND the mechanism is simple to the point of being physics.

Sufficient net flow must bend the price toward itself—the more you buy, the more expensive you make what you are buying; the more you sell, the cheaper you sell it. Impact cost is not friction, it is **the shadow of mass**: past a certain size a position can no longer hide its projection on price, any more than a gravitational field can hide a star. Execution algorithms can slice a hundred-billion position into crumbs, randomize the rhythm, spread it across weeks—**slicing hides the rhythm, it cannot hide the net direction.** To build, you must net buy. Net buying must lift the waterline. This is the life sentence the matching engine passes on every large body.

From which footprints come in three readable shapes. **The first, displacement of net direction**—sustained one-way flow develops on the medium horizon as autocorrelation in the trend, the tally marks left on the chart by the tides and amplifiers of Chapter Nineteen, and the daily bread of every trend follower: you do not need to know who the whale is, only to bet that a net flow already under way is probably not finished. **The second, abnormal persistence**—ordinary volatility comes and goes, but the pressure of an execution flow will not leave. One direction absorbed and pushed, repeatedly and patiently, means somebody is working to a schedule. **The third, distortion of relationships**—a spread that ought to be welded shut cracks open and does not close, which was exactly IG9's tell. When two things that should be equivalent stay persistently unequal, do not begin by suspecting that the law of arbitrage has failed. **Begin by suspecting that something enormous is lying on one side of it.** Those three traces are the small player's free sonar.

And the second half of the story reveals the second consequence of leaving traces, which is also the door into the next chapter: **once identified, the giant's predicament itself becomes the prey.** The hunters' arithmetic was cold. Either the whale keeps feeding the position—and one day it can feed it no longer; or it starts to get out—and every step out delivers the price into the hunters' hands. **Whichever road it takes, it is acting on a have-to**—and somebody else's have-to is your certainty. The most dramatic thing about the London Whale is this: it wanted to disappear, and the only way it could disappear was to become smaller and slower—**and becoming smaller and slower was precisely what its size and its mandate would not allow.** Chapter Seventeen's verdict is confirmed all over again: every weapon is also a shackle on the one who holds it. The whale's weapon was its bulk, and so was its cell.

* * *

PUSH THIS CERTAINTY DOWNWARD AND YOU GET THREE COROLLARIES.

One: the physical foundation of the medium-horizon trend is laid on this certainty. Big money cannot fill in one go → it has to spread out over time → spreading out manufactures measurable persistence on the fifteen-minute to daily scale. This is not mystical momentum, it is the execution flow developing. Trend traders get asked constantly what makes them think that a thing which has gone up will keep going up. The standard answer is in this chapter: **because the flow that pushed the price up here is probably not done executing, and footprints halfway along usually mean the road is halfway along too.**

Two: install the three sonars on your dashboard. Net-direction displacement, read in the structure of the trend. Abnormal persistence, read in how patient the one-way pressure is. Relational distortion, read in bases and spreads—wherever something that should converge keeps diverging, assume a giant first and consider other explanations second. All three instruments are free, all their readings are public, and the only cost is knowing to look at them. If the price is bent, there is mass there. **You cannot see the whale, but you can always see the waterline.**

Three: do not become the whale—including the small edition. This certainty applies to you too; only the pool has been converted. In a thinly traded instrument your modest capital is the whale: your entry drives up your own cost, your stop level glitters on other people's sonar, your exit hands the price to your counterparty. **Size is always relative to the pool.** Past some fraction of that market's depth you stop being a reader of footprints and become a maker of them. The big fish in the small pond dies exactly the way the London Whale died, word for word. Nobody writes it a three-hundred-page report.

That IG9 spread converged in the end, at a cost of $6.2 billion —the law of Chapter Three was late, but it was not absent. And the legacy the case left the whole market fits on one line: **the market never needs to know the whale's name. It only needs to see the waterline.** Mass cannot be made invisible. Position large enough, the price must bend; the price bends, the hunters arrive. As for what exactly it is the hunters carry off—the whale's have-tos—that is the reckoning of the next chapter.

(End of Chapter Twenty)

CHAPTER TWENTY-ONE

Have-To

Certainty 21: Every tier's alpha comes from the constraints of the tier above it—the whole food chain eats other people's have-tos.

TWENTY-ONE CHAPTERS IN, IT IS TIME TO STOP AND TOTAL THE ledger.

The chapters behind us are crowded with winners: the market maker with 1,237 wins and one loss, the trend fund that rode the tide and ate for a whole year, the hedge funds that tracked the waterline to hunt a whale, the exchange that raised margin six days early, and the tax partner who has never once missed a profitable year. Call them all back onto the stage and ask a single question—**where does each winner's money actually come from?**

Nobody in a market pays willingly. No one wakes up and decides to donate a spread to a market maker today. Every steadily flowing stream of money runs down the same buried channel: **from the people with a have-to, to the people without one.** Follow that channel, and walk the food chain again from the top.

Market makers collect on the whole market's have-to-trade-now. Anyone who wants to buy this instant, sell this instant—rather than post an order and wait—must cross the spread.

Each of Virtu's 1,237 profitable days was assembled out of countless people who could not wait: stops cannot wait, margin calls cannot wait, panic cannot wait, and greed cannot wait either. **Hurry is the most widely paid rent in the market.**

Trend funds collect on the inability of sovereign and policy flows to reposition quickly. Money at tidal scale turns in quarters—not because it does not want to be quick, but because a hundred-billion-dollar body physically cannot be (Chapter Nineteen). The part of the turn that never gets finished is the long wake dragging across the surface, and the entire business of the CTAs is to put a price on that wake.

The footprint-readers of the medium and short term collect on big money's inability to execute without a trace. Whales must slice, must spread out, must trudge through time (Chapter Twenty)—and the persistence that spreading creates is precisely the inertia you can bet on in the fifteen-minute chart. The whale hunters charge a crueler rent still: they charge the whale for **its situation itself**—either you go on feeding, or you begin to back out, and both roads run through me.

Carry players collect on central banks having to keep their policy promises—the differential hangs there because each of two central banks has something of its own it cannot move (the calendar of Chapter Five draws its third paycheck here). **Exchanges and brokers** collect on everyone's have-to-come-through-me—an institutional toll, paid in drought and flood alike. And at the very top of the chain sits the partner from Chapter Six: **the revenue service collects on your have-to-settle**—even a winner's money must queue at that gate in the end.

Now see the first thing this picture means: **it is not a pyramid ranked by intelligence.** The market maker is no smarter than the CTA, the whale hunter no smarter than the whale—each tier can collect rent for exactly one reason, that it happens not to be wearing the shackle the tier above wears. The second meaning is colder: **almost no tier only eats and is never eaten.** Market makers take a toll from the whole floor and get bitten by better-informed order flow (they have to keep quoting; that is their shackle). CTAs eat the tide and get slapped by sovereign ambush and poisoned by their own crowding (Chapter Fifteen). Whales eat the dividend of size and are betrayed by their own volume. Every seat is a place at the table and a dish on it—**the only stable net collector of rent is the structure itself**: the platform, the rules, the tax. Which buckles this chapter to the finding of Chapter Four: certain income all grows on the rule side.

* * *

Now the threads buried through the first two parts can be gathered in one pull.

Part One inventoried the certainties of rules and costs, Part Two the certainties of mathematics. At the time they looked like a manual for surviving disasters. Only here does their second identity show: **every certainty is somebody's shackle, and every shackle is somebody else's source of rent.** Settlement rules are certain (Chapter Five) → the carry trader collects rent on them. Execution always leaves a trace (Chapter Twenty) → the trend follower collects rent on that. Margin arithmetic is certain (Chapter Twelve) → the hunters of forced liquidation collect rent on it. The stop mechanism is certain (Chapter Two) → someone collects rent on where the stops sit, which is the subject of the next several chapters. Even the certainty that human discipline is unreliable (Chapter Sixteen) feeds an entire industry devoted to inducing trades. **The reason this book spent twenty chapters counting certainties is that it was drawing a rent map**—where there is certainty, there is a shackle; where there is a shackle, that is where the money runs past.

So the old question that has run through the whole book—out of whose pocket, and for what reason, does this money come into yours—can be upgraded now to its final form:

Whose have-to does this money come from, and which one?

If you can answer, and that have-to is structural—written into a mandate, into a charter, into physics—you hold a lease that can be renewed. If you cannot answer—**assume you are the one paying rent.**

Finally, the bottom of the chain. Why is retail food over the long run? The popular answers—not enough money, news too slow, weak technique—all miss. What matters is the thing almost nobody says out loud: **retail is the only species on the entire food chain whose have-tos are not imposed by structure but invented by itself.** The market maker has to quote: charter. The fund has to stay fully invested: mandate. The whale has to spread out: physics. And the retail have-tos—have to watch the screen every day, have to win the loss back, have to find a trade when bored, have to be fully loaded or it feels wasted—**not one of them is written in any document. Every one was fitted on by the wearer.** The whole market collects rent on those homemade shackles: the spread collects, slippage collects, the event window collects, the stop hunters collect, the tax collects. Retail is not born prey. Retail is prey **by voluntary declaration.**

* * *

PUSH THIS CERTAINTY DOWNWARD AND YOU GET THREE COROLLARIES.

One: write a statement of rent source for every strategy you run. One sentence, in this form: this strategy collects rent on ____'s have-to ____; the constraint exists by virtue of ____ (mandate / rule / physics); the constraint is released when ____. That third clause is the one worth money—it is the death monitor on your edge. While the constraint stands, the lease stands; when the constraint is released, the strategy dies. The good news is that the hardest constraints are close to perpetual: as long as big money still has to build positions, net direction cannot be hidden (Chapter Twenty), and the ground under that lease runs deeper than most edges ever go.

Two: audit the list of rents you are paying right now. Line by line: spread rent, on every trade; event rent, if you do not filter the windows; overnight rent; location rent, for a stop parked where everybody parks theirs; tax rent; and the most expensive line of all—**behavior rent**: every trade set off by a self-made have-to. Chapter Four said that trading less is a direct source of profit. Now it has a unified theory. **What you are giving up is not trades, it is shackles you invented yourself**—and every one you take off shrinks the surface area available to rent.

Three: cutting your have-to list to zero is the one project retail can finish and an institution never can. An institution's shackles are welded into its charter, and removing one takes a board. Yours are all habits, and removing one takes an evening. Which implies something the industry deliberately declines to discuss: **climbing this food chain is not a matter of getting stronger, it is a matter of leaving nothing to bite**—however good the rent collector's aim, he cannot hit a target with no have-to on it. And when your list really does reach zero, you will be holding something nobody else on the chain has. What it is, the last chapter of this book will say.

The ledger can be closed here. The bottom line is one sentence, and it is where this book got its title: **the only certainties in trading are your costs and other people's have-tos.** Your costs are the rent you are certain to pay. Other people's have-tos are the only rent you could ever collect. Debit and credit—that is the whole account of a trading life.

(End of Chapter Twenty-One)

Chapter Twenty-Two

One Window Each

Certainty 22: No participant can see the complete order book—not even the market makers. Price is the only information everyone shares, no one can hide, and everyone gets free.

In June 2014, the Attorney General of New York, Eric Schneiderman, filed a complaint. The defendant was Barclays.

The case was simple enough. Barclays ran what was then the second-largest dark pool in the United States—a private venue that publishes no quotes and exists to match institutional blocks, trading under the name LX. The sales pitch was safety: we run surveillance, we identify and restrain "predatory" high-frequency traders, and in here you can stay clear of the sharks of the public market. The marketing material even included a chart breaking down who was swimming in the pool. All above board, nobody cheated.

What the complaint established was this: **the chart had been retouched by hand—the largest high-frequency participant in the pool, the one Barclays' own internal documents labeled "toxic," had been deleted from it.** And the protection mechanism had never actually kept anyone out; on the contrary, to build volume, Barclays was privately courting the very sharks it publicly promised to exclude. The Attorney General's summing-up was hard enough to cut into stone: Barclays grew its dark pool by telling investors they were diving into safe waters—and according to the complaint, the pool was full of predators, **there at Barclays' invitation.**

The case closed in 2016. Barclays paid $70 million, admitted misleading investors and violating securities law, and accepted an independent monitor; Credit Suisse, charged in parallel over its own pool, paid $84.3 million. Together, $154.3 million—the largest penalties in the history of dark pool enforcement.

The case normally gets filed in the drawer marked "bank lies again." For this book its value lies a layer down: **even the swimmers in the dark pool could not see the water in their own pool.** They had nothing to go on but the map the owner handed out, and the map had been edited. If a single pool cannot take an honest census of itself, what about the whole ocean?

* * *

THE ANSWER IS THIS CHAPTER'S CERTAINTY, AND IT IS WORTH enumerating item by item, because nearly every trader has the opposite superstition living inside his head.

US equity volume is scattered across a dozen-odd public exchanges, dozens of dark pools, and a great deal of broker internalization that never touches any "book" at all—**around forty percent of trading happens outside every public order book**; no venue and no machine holds the complete picture at any one moment. A public exchange sees only its own book. A dark pool sees only its own water—and, as we have just seen, even the census the owner supplies may be fiction. An iceberg order keeps its size below the surface and shows a corner on the book. Foreign exchange is more thorough still: **it has no central order book at all.** That convincing-looking "depth" on your platform is the slice which the handful of liquidity providers your broker happens to connect to are willing to display to this particular pool; out of the window at the broker next door lies a completely different landscape. The market makers? They see only the portion of order flow that runs through them. The regulators? They spend years afterwards stitching audit trails together, and what they stitch is still fragments.

So the popular superstition can be formally buried: **the idea that "the big players," "the house," can see everything—no such being exists.** There is no omniscient party in this market, only a few million windows of different sizes. Virtu's window is larger, yours is smaller, and the institutions in the Barclays pool believed theirs was clean—**every one of them guessing at the shape of the whole ocean through his own pane.** The error in the conspiracy theory is not the suspicion. It is that it misreads a structure as a personality. Your fear is entitled to exist, but it should be posted to the right address: your broker really can see everything about **you** (an account settled in a chapter of its own further on); but nobody at all can see everything about **everybody**.

Then there is the other face of this certainty, and it is the gift the certainty makes to the small player.

Every window is partial, but one thing shines into all of them: **the traded price.** A resting order can be canceled, disguised, shown as a tip of ice, withdrawn from you at the last instant—a resting order is a performance of intent. **A trade is a fact somebody has paid for.** Every execution leaves its mark on the tape, and the net effect of all executions—the movement of price—is public information, shared by the whole market at the same instant, free, and impossible to deny after the fact. The iceberg can hide the volume under the water; it cannot hide how the waterline changed once it traded. The dark pool can hide the matching; the trade still has to report to the tape. Chapter Twenty said you cannot see the whale but you can see the waterline. This chapter supplies the epistemology under it: **the waterline can be trusted precisely because it is the one reading nobody can forge alone.** The people paying a fortune for a bigger window are buying a larger sample of guesses about intent. The people watching the waterline are reading the result itself.

* * *

PUSH THIS CERTAINTY DOWNWARD AND YOU GET THREE COROLLARIES.

One: post your fear to the right address. "Someone can see my stop"—make it precise: your broker can see it, the market cannot. "The big players are watching me"—that sentence has no subject. Once the fear is precise, the countermeasure is obvious: against the broker, the counterparty management of Chapter Seven and the discipline of placement in the chapters ahead; against the omniscient being that does not exist, the only correct action is to stop modifying your system on its behalf. **Sacrificing to a god who is not there is the most common religious expense in retail trading.**

Two: order book information may be used, but only at the grade of a local sample. The DOM is your window—look at it, and keep track of where the frame is. Depth across venues cannot be added up. A resting order is not a promise. Signals built on resting orders are fragile by nature, because resting orders are free and cancellable: that is a data set in which everyone can lie and lying costs nothing. Signals built on executions carry a deposit—whoever said that sentence has already paid for it. From which follows a corollary that saves money: do not pay the arms tax for a bigger window (the procurement-list principle of Chapter Seventeen). However big the window, it is still a window.

Three: lay the foundation of your system on the traded price. Backtests, signals, validation—anchor every one of them to executions and displacement, and demote the quote stream to instrumentation: the spread as a breathing monitor (Chapter Eighteen), depth as a reference, **executions alone as fact.** One line of fine print, for honesty: Chapter Eight said that even the trade record can be brushed by the eraser on extreme days. But that is a rare exceptional remedy. Under normal conditions, price displacement remains the hardest public fact in this market, with nothing in second place. If not that, then what?

Back to the retouched pool. Its real lesson is not that dark pools are dark—**it is that even the man selling the window cannot see the whole of it, and lies about the part he can.** In a market where every person has exactly one window, rather than save up for a better one, remember the light that reaches all of them: the traded price, exact to the tick, free of charge, the same for everyone. **The man watching the waterline never has to buy a window.**

(End of Chapter Twenty-Two)

CHAPTER TWENTY-THREE

Information That Does Not Exist Yet

Certainty 23: History is completely visible and intent is completely invisible—everything you can see is "already executed," and you never see "about to execute".

EVERY DECEMBER, WALL STREET PERFORMS A RITUAL THAT nothing on earth can cancel.

Goldman Sachs, Morgan Stanley, Bank of America—the chief strategists of the major banks publish their annual outlooks, giving a target level for the S&P 500 **twelve months out**. These are the most expensive brains the industry can hire, backed by the fullest data, the fastest information, and the largest of the windows in Chapter Twenty-Two. Their forecasts get quoted by funds, repeated by the press, and treated by countless investors as the map of the year to come.

Now go to the archive. Researchers have lined up the Wall Street consensus for every year since 2000 against what actually happened twelve months later. The result: **in twenty-five years, the consensus has forecast a rise every single year**, an average predicted gain of about 9%. In fact, seven of those years closed down. In a quarter of a century, **Wall Street has never once forecast a down year.** The average gap between forecast and outcome is 14.2 percentage points. The worst samples: in 2008 the consensus called for +9.2% and the market fell 38.5%, a miss of nearly fifty points; in 2022, +3.9% against an actual −19.4%; and then in 2023 and 2024, two years running, they missed two rallies of more than 20% in the other direction. A separate study tallied the directional calls of well-known market experts and put overall accuracy at **47%—worse than a coin.**

The first reaction is usually mockery: these people are hopeless. The second is conspiracy: they talk it up to bring in clients. Neither reaction lands. **These forecasters are not stupid, and mostly not dishonest either. They are answering a question whose answer nobody holds.**

* * *

THINK ABOUT WHERE THE ANSWER TO "WHAT WILL THE MARKET DO next year" is being kept at this moment.

Not in any vault, not on any server, not in a drawer at the Federal Reserve—because **it has not been manufactured yet.** Next year's prices will be cast out of hundreds of millions of decisions not yet made, and at this moment those decisions are "nonexistent" in three separate ways.

First, they are scattered across a few million brains and a few million servers, with no central repository—and that is merely a problem of collection. **Second, the overwhelming majority of them are conditional**: if it drops to X I sell, if volatility goes above Y I cut, if the central bank turns I flip long. Even the person holding the intention could not give you an unconditional version of it; scan his brain and what you extract is a tree hung with ifs. **Third, and deepest: the conditions themselves will keep being rewritten by future prices—**

tomorrow's version of him will be another man, made so by tomorrow's market. (That rewriting machine gets taken apart in full in the finale.)

So throw away a popular metaphor. Future order flow is not **a card lying face down on the table**; a face-down card has already been printed, you simply cannot see it. Future order flow is **a card that has not been printed.** Chapter Twenty-Two said you cannot see all of the present order book: that is a window problem—the information exists, your pane is small. This chapter is about something else entirely: **future intent is invisible because of a problem of existence. It is not hidden. It is not yet.** A window problem can be eased with money; an existence problem cannot be eased by any sum at all. Which is why the most expensive brains plus the largest windows sat the exam for twenty-five years and scored below a coin. The lock on the market's unpredictability now has two tumblers: **the present cannot be seen whole, and the future does not exist.** (The third is saved for the finale.)

Once this certainty stands, it flattens two foundations and pours a new one.

First demolition: every strategy has exactly one raw material—the past. Technical analysis uses past prices. Fundamental analysis uses past filings: a financial statement is a historical document, and news is the past that has only just arrived. Quantitative models eat everything that has already happened. Nobody is trading the future. **Some people merely narrate the past so that it sounds like the future.** There is no shame in admitting this. The shame is in not admitting it: you and the Goldman strategist and the deepest quant fund hold identical inventories of raw material, and the only differences are in the processing and in the honesty.

Second demolition: anyone claiming to know what will happen is either lying or describing a statistical tendency without knowing it. There is no third possibility—the answer does not exist, so nobody claiming to hold it can be holding it honestly. This is the counterfeit filter the book is giving you; how to use it is in the corollaries.

The new foundation: intent is invisible, but execution already under way has inertia. This is the joint between this chapter and Chapter Twenty, and it is the only source of legitimacy statistical betting has. You never know what a whale **wants** to do; but the half it **has already done** physically entails the half it has not. A hundred-billion build that has reached thirty percent leaves seventy percent that is not intent at all but **a liability already contracted.** A footprint is not a leak of what somebody is thinking. A footprint is a promissory note. Betting that the note gets honored takes no mind reading, only the reading of physics. That is the line between the prophet and the statistician: the prophet bets on something that does not exist, the statistician bets on the inertia of something that does.

* * *

Push this certainty downward and you get three corollaries.

One: install a grammar filter, on other people first and then on yourself. When you listen to any analysis, any signal source, any famous name, listen only to the grammar. "Will break out," "is bound to reach," "target X"—prophet grammar, the answer does not exist, downgrade the source or block it. "Historically, after this pattern, it continued 60% of the time," "the odds lean," "if A then B"—statistician grammar, keep listening. Then turn the filter on yourself. Open your trading journal and count the prophet sentences—*this is definitely bouncing here*—and rewrite them one at a time as statistical sentences. Your system will get a great deal more honest overnight. **Grammar betrays how you think, and how you think decides how you die.**

Two: convert the unanswerable question into an answerable one. "Will it go up?"—that answer lives in the future, nobody holds it, and whoever answers is making it up. "Does the shape of the last twenty candles look more like the continuation of an execution flow, or like its exhaustion?"—that answer lives in data that already exists, and can be given honestly. **The grammar of the question decides the quality of the answer.** Ask analysts this way, ask indicators this way, ask anything that calls itself intelligent this way, and above all ask yourself this way when you review. A trader can very nearly be graded on the grammar of his questions.

Three: write plans as condition trees, not as scripts. Since the future is cast out of hundreds of millions of conditional intentions, the shape of plan that matches the market is not "tomorrow it reaches X and I buy at Y"—a script is destined to be humiliated by reality—but a tree grown in the same shape as everybody else's intentions: if A, do one; if B, do two; if neither, do nothing. You cannot read anyone's conditional orders, **but you can turn yourself into a conditional machine as well**—never predicting which card gets printed, only guaranteeing that whichever one comes out, your reply was written long ago.

The December ritual will continue, the forecasts will go on failing, the banks will go on publishing—because what the client is buying has never been accuracy. It is the comfort of a future that exists and can be known. This book cannot sell that comfort. All it can hand you is the cold dividing line:

everything that has happened is entirely public; everything that will happen is entirely blank. The whole craft of trading is to stand on that line, use only the material on the left, and bet on the right. The line is called now.

(End of Chapter Twenty-Three)

CHAPTER TWENTY-FOUR

Developing

Certainty 24: Forecast accuracy decays asymmetrically across time scales —at a point in time you know nothing; stretch the scale and a statistical tendency begins to develop. But what develops is always a distribution, never a direction.

RUN A THREE-QUESTION EXPERIMENT. ONE MARKET—SAY EUR/USD—and three questions.

Question one: the next tick, up or down? The honest answer is that nobody knows. Nobody on earth. And do not rush to say the high-frequency firms know: Virtu, in Chapter Seventeen, is the proof of the opposite. It posts on the bid and the offer at the same moment, **precisely because it does not know which way the next tick goes**, which is why it stands on both sides. It earns the spread, not the direction. At tick scale, price is set by market makers adjusting inventory, by games inside the queue, by orders arriving at random—a pure sea of noise, where you and a pair of dice are kin.

Question two: the next fifteen minutes? Now there is a little to be said—**if** a whale happens to be executing (Chapter Twenty). The net flow that has already moved the price has probably not finished, and the probability of continuation is lifted a few percentage points. Note the wording. Not "it will rise," but "the probability of continuation may have gone from 50% to 55%." A measurable, minute tilt.

Question three: the next quarter? Suppose the Fed is in a hiking cycle while another central bank is holding its rate down (the tide of Chapter Nineteen). Then the distribution of returns over that quarter is **visibly skewed to one side**: the direction of the differential works like a slope, tipping the whole histogram of outcomes. And still nobody can tell you which day it rises, how far it goes, or what the path looks like—and do not forget that a five-yen sovereign slap took place on that same slope.

Set the three answers side by side and this chapter's certainty appears: **from tick to quarter, the amount that can be known increases—but what increases has never been direction. It is the degree of tilt in the distribution.** And the decay structure itself is stable and can be relied on: what is knowable at each scale is decided by the structure of the market, not by how clever you happen to be.

* * *

WHY? THE MECHANISM IS AS CLEAN AS A PHYSICS PROBLEM.

Every jump in price is the superposition of two components. **Noise**—the market maker's inventory swinging back, the bounce between bid and offer, the impact of a random order. And **flow**—sustained net pressure in one direction: execution flow, tides. Noise has one fatal property: it holds no grudge, its sign is random, and stretch out the time and the pieces cancel one another; sum a thousand random bounces and the ups and downs very nearly annul. Flow is the opposite: it holds a grudge, its direction persists, and stretched out in time it **accumulates linearly**. So at short scales the volume of noise drowns out everything and what you hear is pure hiss; stretch the scale, the noise cancels itself, and the melody of the flow surfaces —

This is developing. A long exposure in a darkroom: one photon landing on the film is nothing at all, but the longer the exposure, the more photons accumulate, and an outline emerges out of the grain. Expose this market's film for a minute and you have specks; for fifteen minutes and there is a faint shape; for a quarter and the outline of the tide is legible. But the camera carries a curse of its own, and that curse is the second half of this chapter's certainty: **what it develops is always a greyscale map of probability, and there are no arrows on it.** Expose it as long as you like and all you obtain is a histogram that leans right—and inside that leaning distribution sit seven losses in a row (Chapter Eleven), the hammer blow of an intervention day (Chapter Nineteen), and every path that will make you doubt your own existence. The tilt is real. The promise does not exist.

While we are here, the strategists of Chapter Twenty-Three can be half acquitted. Forecasting +9% every year is not entirely wrong—**that is roughly the historical base rate of the stock market**, most years really do rise, and as a statement about a distribution it is perfectly legitimate. Their crime is to have traced a greyscale image into an arrow, to have packaged "the distribution leans upward over the long run" as "X points by the end of next year." However sharply the distribution develops, the level is still invented—**that the distribution is knowable and the path is not can both be true at once, and always are.**

Line the earlier cast up by scale, and the food chain suddenly shows another kind of order. **The tick layer is where the market makers live**—they forecast nothing, and turn noise into rent by quoting both sides. **The minute-to-hour layer is where the readers of execution flow live**—they harvest the persistence created by whales spreading their footprints out. **The week-to-month layer is where trend and macro players live**—they put a price on the tide. **At the scale of a year there is nothing left but the base rate**—the territory of buy and hold. High frequency competes on speed, low frequency on statistics, and the middle floors on the developing of execution flow. Chapter Seventeen said each king is locked inside his own dimension; this chapter supplies the coordinates: **each of them is locked inside a length of exposure.** And the point in time—exactly when—develops at no scale whatever. It is the last residue in the noise, the part that never cancels, and anyone who claims to command it goes straight into the filter of Chapter Twenty-Three.

* * *

PUSH THIS CERTAINTY DOWNWARD AND YOU GET THREE COROLLARIES.

One: choosing your timeframe is choosing your exposure time, and there is a first-principles method for it. The floor is drawn by cost: Chapter Four ran the arithmetic, and cost as a share of expected profit climbs steeply as the period shortens—expose too briefly and the whole plate develops into rent paid to the green square. The ceiling is drawn by your capital and by structure: the arms map of Chapter Seventeen marks which exposure bands are crowded with armed men. Your optimal period is the middle floor where **execution flow develops clearly, cost is a negligible share, and the heavily armed cannot reach you.** There is exactly one test: at the scale you have chosen, is the tilt in your signal statistically measurable? If it is not, either change the exposure or admit you have no signal.

Two: write every expectation in your system in the language of distributions. What a signal hands you is not a target price but a set of three: the tilt (win rate and payoff), the expected value, and the number of samples required to confirm the tilt is still there. A take-profit is not a forecast—**it is a harvest line drawn on a distribution.** A stop is not an opinion—it is the budget you have set for the left tail (Chapter Eleven). The instant you say to yourself "this one is going to X," you have slid from statistician to prophet; the filter sounds once, and you fine yourself one rewrite.

Three: the point in time never develops, so entries must be zones and conditions, never moments. The exact high and the exact low live on the layer that never develops, and any system that has to catch that one candle to make money has its foundation in noise. It will die; only the speed is in question. The workable version: write the entry as a price zone plus a trigger condition, allow yourself to scale in, tolerate imperfection. **You are working on a greyscale image, and the tool for that is a brush, not a needle.**

The three-question experiment can be closed. The tick yields nothing, fifteen minutes yields a trace of tilt, a quarter yields a field of slanted gray—and at no level whatever do you get an arrow. Whoever demands a direction from the market will wait his whole life for the reply; whoever learns to read greyscale eats at every exposure. **The developer is time—and time develops nothing but distributions.**

(End of Chapter Twenty-Four)

Chapter Twenty-Five

Starlight

Certainty 25: Latency is necessarily greater than zero—you are always trading against the past.

Look up at the sun and you are not looking at the sun.

You are looking at the sun of eight minutes ago—light that left its surface and ran a hundred and fifty million kilometres to reach your retina. The night sky is worse. Some of that starlight has been traveling four years, some of it several thousand; what you gaze up at is never "the sky right now," it is a collage in time, pieced together out of old light from different eras. Astronomers file no complaint about this, because the rule admits no exception: **information takes time to travel, and time makes exceptions for no one.**

Now look down at your quote screen.

That flickering number is the same substance as starlight. It is born on some liquidity provider's server, dives into fibre—light in glass runs at two-thirds of its speed in vacuum, about half a millisecond for every hundred kilometres—passes through aggregation, routing, the rendering engine of your platform, and finally leaves the screen as photons and lands on your retina. By then it is already **a price from tens to hundreds of milliseconds ago.** And that is only the outbound leg. Your eye hands it to your brain; human neural response takes upward of two hundred milliseconds, and subjective hesitation is measured in whole seconds. You click, the order runs the road back, queues at the matching engine, waits to be filled. Add up the chain end to end: for a manual trader, between "the price happens" and "the order lands" there is **a gap measured in seconds.**

During that gap the market did not wait for you. What you get filled against is never the market you saw—**it is that market's descendant.**

Every link in the chain takes strictly more than zero, and the seal on it is physical law, not insufficiently advanced technology: the speed of light is the universe's limit, nerve conduction is biology's limit, the matching queue is the institution's limit. That three-hundred-million-dollar cable in Chapter Three bought nothing more than shortening the past from sixteen milliseconds to thirteen; the ones who came after used microwave to squeeze it to eight. **Nobody has ever bought zero.** Academics have run the arithmetic in earnest: once the speed of light binds, the optimal server location for cross-market arbitrage sits in the middle of the ocean. When relativity starts participating in site selection, you should understand what class of certainty this is: **you are always trading against the past, everyone is, and the only difference is whether your photograph is a few microseconds old or a few seconds old.**

* * *

THAT OLD PHOTOGRAPH APPEARS ON YOUR STATEMENT UNDER TWO names.

The first name is slippage. You decide on the price you saw and you are filled at the price when the order arrived—and the difference between the two is exactly **the distance the market traveled inside your latency.** In quiet hours the market barely moves in a few hundred milliseconds, the invoice comes to approximately zero, and you conclude that latency does not exist. In a fast market, those same few hundred milliseconds can cover the ground the market usually covers in an hour—the Swiss franc in Chapter Two, the yen in Chapter One; those horrifying slippage numbers are all, at bottom, the same invoice. **The latency did not change. What changed was the market's speed inside it.** One item for later: there is a class of counterparty that exploits your latency perfectly legally—on receiving your order it takes one more look at the current market, and if the move has gone against it, refuses the fill; if the move has gone its way, takes the whole thing. The name of that mechanism, and its full accounting, is settled in Chapter Twenty-Seven.

The second name is the native optimism of the backtest. Every backtest report defaults to filling at the signal price—translated: **it assumes latency is zero, it assumes you live in the market's now.** Nobody lives there. The seam between the signal price and the real fill does not exist in the backtest and exists on every single live trade; and the share of expected profit that seam consumes grows as the timeframe shortens. For a swing trade targeting a hundred pips, a few hundred milliseconds of staleness is dust. For a scalp grabbing a few pips, it is life and death. Put the green square of Chapter Four and the seam of time in this chapter on the same page, and you have the complete autopsy report on why the short timeframes are carpeted with bodies.

But this certainty comes with an exemption built into it, and the exemption is issued specifically to the small player: **the cost of staleness is inversely proportional to your holding period.** For a trade you intend to hold three days, a two-hundred-millisecond photograph is stale in no meaningful sense—the age of the picture divided by the length of the hold is approximately zero. This is another load-bearing column under the middle floor of Chapter Twenty-Four: the high-frequency crowd lives in the speed-of-light district, where the rent is charged by the millisecond; once you have chosen your exposure time, latency is **free** to you. If you cannot beat the speed of light, do not live on its street. Move far enough out and the speed of light becomes your city wall: any game that only stands up with a reaction measured in seconds is barred from your door by physics—and barred along with it is everyone who wanted to lure you into that race.

* * *

PUSH THIS CERTAINTY DOWNWARD AND YOU GET THREE COROLLARIES.

One: measure the age of your own photograph. Do not guess. Measure: your platform's round-trip latency; the timestamps in the execution report—signal time, submit time, fill time, three columns, into your forward log (the execution log of Chapter Sixteen; add these three columns); and once a month, look at the distribution of your slippage—**the tail, not the mean** (the old rule from Chapter Fourteen). Most people know nothing whatsoever about the latency of their own system and hold abundant opinions about the direction of the market. The order is reversed: the first is measurable and fixable, the second is unknowable.

Two: a backtest must price latency. Inject your measured slippage distribution—tail included—into the backtest; model the event windows (Chapter Eighteen) separately, because the invoice there runs five to ten times normal. Then execute the familiar verdict: **double the slippage assumption, and if the strategy dies, the strategy is already dead**—it simply has not yet received the invoice the live market put in the post.

Three: run a matching audit between timeframe and latency. Compute one number: your end-to-end latency ÷ your average holding time. That staleness ratio should be small enough to ignore. If it cannot be, there are two roads: stretch the timeframe until latency stops mattering, or admit that this game requires infrastructure you cannot afford (the procurement principle of Chapter Seventeen: enough and no more, not one millisecond extra). And after the audit passes, one more piece of discipline: **do not let the intraday version of you reintroduce latency sensitivity**—a system designed in days, with you sitting there itching over second-by-second wiggles, is you volunteering to rent back on the speed-of-light street.

The astronomers' attitude is worth copying out wholesale. They never complain that starlight is old; they made the oldness itself into an instrument. The further out they look, the older the universe they see—an entire discipline is built on that delay. A trader's maturity begins with the same move: admit that every price on your screen is starlight, and then **build your reason for making money on something that outlives your latency**—the inertia of execution flow runs in hours, the tides run in months, and your latency runs in milliseconds. You cannot live in the market's now. Fortunately, making money never required it.

(End of Chapter Twenty-Five)

Chapter Twenty-Six

Where the Inventory Comes From

Certainty 26: Every fill must have a counterparty—and the stop cluster is the only large passive counterparty in the market whose existence is certain.

For years a grievance has circulated among retail traders, and professionals laugh at it: "My stop always gets taken out by exactly the wrong tick. Somebody must be hunting stops." The standard reply is a contemptuous smile. Conspiracy theory. Victim mentality. You are not that important.

On November 12, 2014, the UK Financial Conduct Authority issued the largest fine in the history of the City of London—five of the world's top banks, $1.7 billion between them; add the American and Swiss regulators' penalties the same day and the total came to $4.3 billion. In the notices, the regulators set out in their own words what these banks' FX traders had done. One count reads, verbatim: they shared confidential client order information and then "**attempted to manipulate fix rates and trigger client stop loss orders**."

Not an insinuation, not an inference—a regulatory finding, in black and white, with the chat logs attached. Those traders worked in concert in invitation-only chat rooms, and the names of the rooms were all made public afterwards: "the players";

"the 3 musketeers," one of whose members contributed a line that went straight into the notice—"we all die together"; "1 team, 1 dream"; and the most famous of them, from the EU's later fines, "the cartel." In May 2015 the story reached its legal terminus: several banks **pleaded guilty to criminal charges** over FX manipulation, adding more than five billion dollars in fines. The retail grievance, it turns out, has a case number in the regulatory archive.

But sit down, because the conspiracy is not what this chapter is about. **The conspiracy is the smallest part of this story.** Chat rooms can be shut down and traders can be prosecuted. The machine they were exploiting can be neither fined nor arrested, because the overwhelming bulk of it is entirely legal, and it grows in the bones of the market.

* * *

Back to the old question of Chapter Twenty-One: in this market, who has to?

Now ask it from the other end. A whale that needs to buy two billion (Chapter Twenty)—what is its hardest problem? Not the money. **The counterparty.** It needs to find someone willing to sell two billion at this moment and at this price, and preferably without running the price away from itself. Chapter Twenty-Two said it: a resting order is a performance of intent, cancellable at any instant. Almost every "seller" in the market is a **maybe**—maybe I'll sell, depends on the price, let me think about it.

Only one kind of seller is **certain.**

The stop order. What is a long's stop, in its legal nature? Chapter Two dissected it: **triggered, it is a market order—no**

price limit, immediate execution. It is a pre-signed, unconditional promise to sell, hanging there in black and white with its trigger price stated on its face, in all weathers. And they are not scattered at random: human beings learned the same rules out of the same textbooks—put the stop below the prior low, put it behind the round number—so ten million promises to sell **pile up at a handful of levels anybody can compute**, stacked as neatly as a warehouse.

Now finish the whale's arithmetic, and notice that it is nothing but the arithmetic of profit: **chase profit → you must count costs → costs are lowest where the other side is thickest → and the thickest other side, the only one certain to be present, is the stop cluster.** Push price a few pips through the prior low and the first layer trips—market sell orders come pouring out—take them, press again, trip the second layer. A whole warehouse of inventory, delivered to the buyer in bulk, at descending prices, inside a few seconds. Then the purchasing is done, and price comes back.

So revise the grievance into its adult form: **retail stops are not hunted for sport—they are where somebody's inventory comes from.** "Hunting" implies malice and games. The truth is colder: nobody hates you, your stop simply happens to appear on a shopping list. The cartel's crime was peeking at the warehouse inventory sheet in advance (the confidential client orders). The existence of the warehouse, the predictability of its location, and the certain-to-fill nature of its contents require no inside information at all—**anyone who has read the same textbook can work out where you left your promise.** The LME in Chapter Nine, Brexit in Chapter Eighteen, the yen flash crash in Chapter One: every large move has the same fuel in its tanks.

The honest boundary has to be drawn too: **"stop clusters get visited" is a strong structural tendency, not an inevitability every time.** Not every prior low gets swept—the purchasing only happens when large money happens to need inventory nearby. Which means betting the other way, that price always reverses after the sweep, is still a statistical bet and not an arbitrage. This tilt, like every tilt in this book (Chapter Twenty-Four), can be harvested and must not be believed in.

* * *

PUSH THIS CERTAINTY DOWNWARD AND YOU GET THREE COROLLARIES.

One: the anti-obviousness principle of stop placement. Your stop has two functions; design them separately. **Function one is discipline**—it guarantees that you leave, which Chapter Two established. **Function two is location**—it decides whether you are lying on somebody's shopping list. Three to five pips under the prior low, one step behind the round number: that is the bullseye of the cluster, and the textbook standardized it with its own hands. Two remedies. Either put the stop beyond the cluster's range—a wider stop, position size cut in proportion (the formula in Chapter Ten), risk budget unchanged to the penny, and what the money bought was distance from the bullseye. Or switch to a structural stop or a time stop, so the exit condition stops being a price everybody can compute. **A few extra pips of stop width is one of the cheapest insurance policies this market sells.**

Two: learn to autopsy a sweep, and tell the two sequels apart. Price punches through the prior low, and there are only two sequels. **A real break**—the execution flow continues, price never looks back; that is the footprint of Chapter Twenty on the march. **A false break**—a violent snap back, a wick left behind; that is usually the delivery receipt for a completed purchase, and the real direction from there runs opposite to the break. The second is the natural predator of trend systems: you chase the break and it reverses, you flip and you are late, and you take the beating from both ends. Do two things at minimum: recognize it, and do not feed it orders while its mouth is open. Then open your own history of losses and count what proportion of it clusters around this pattern—most trend traders find the fattest single line on their bill sitting right there.

Three: before every stop you place, do the arithmetic for the other side. A ritual question, ten seconds: "If I were large money that needed inventory right now, would this level be on my shopping list?" Yes—move it, or change the exit mechanism. No—place it. This is the rent audit of Chapter Twenty-One carried down to the final centimetre: your stop is a have-to that you wrote out yourself, priced, and filed for public inspection—**the only document in the whole market that publishes your inevitable behavior in advance.** Other people's have-tos are your alpha; of your own, every one you can keep off the register is one saved.

Those chat rooms were shut down long ago, and the traders went to court or changed industries. The machine they hunted with is still running tonight: as long as a stop is a promise that becomes a market order the instant it is touched, the stop cluster remains the only certain block of passive counterparty in the market—**and a certain counterparty will never lack for someone to come and take it.** Regulators can fine a conspiracy. They cannot fine matching. You cannot change this machine.

You have exactly one choice: **do not hang your promise to exit on somebody else's shopping list.**

(End of Chapter Twenty-Six)

Chapter Twenty-Seven

First Reader

Certainty 27: Your order is seen by your broker before it reaches the market—and in the B-book model, your stop is not a secret to it. It is its income statement.

FXCM WAS ONCE THE LARGEST RETAIL FOREIGN EXCHANGE BROKER in the United States, and its gold-lettered sign read three words: **No Dealing Desk.**

The marketing was airtight. We do not take the other side of our clients—your order is routed straight out to a panel of **independent** market makers competing for it; your profit and loss has nothing to do with our profit; we are the messenger passing through, and we take a small toll for the pipe. "No conflict of interest" was written into what the firm called its core philosophy and printed on every brochure. Millions of retail traders chose it for that promise.

On February 6, 2017, an order from the US Commodity Futures Trading Commission opened up the back office. The regulator established that as early as 2009 FXCM had internally commissioned a market-making algorithm and then "spun it off" into an "independent" company named Effex Capital—independent to what degree? Its head was a former managing director of FXCM. Its start-up capital was an **interest-free loan** from FXCM. It operated out of FXCM's offices, using FXCM's staff. And this "independent market maker" proceeded to win, consistently, the largest share of FXCM's client order flow in the competitive auction—**and winning the order flow means standing on the other side of the client.** In return, Effex rebated roughly seventy percent of its trading profits to FXCM every month: from 2010 to 2014, some **$77 million** in total.

In plain language: the platform that swore on its life it would never bet against you was keeping an in-house counterparty, feeding it your orders, and drawing a monthly share of your losses—while lying to the regulator to conceal the relationship. Judgment: a $7 million fine, and FXCM and two of its founders **permanently barred from the US market.** The largest retail FX firm in America, deported. The company promptly changed its name, and the brand went on doing business overseas under another flag.

You are entitled to be angry here. But twenty-seven chapters into this book you can already guess the next sentence: **the scandal is the smallest part of this story.** FXCM's crime was lying. The structure the lie concealed requires no fraud whatsoever to exist, and at this moment it is running underneath every retail account there is.

* * *

DISSECT THE JOURNEY OF ONE OF YOUR ORDERS. YOU CLICK SELL—and the order's first stop is **always** your broker's server. Before any market, before any liquidity provider has laid eyes on it, your broker has already seen it: this order, your stop level, your entire book of positions, your equity and margin level, every trade in your history, and the **behavioural profile** that has

GROWN OUT OF THAT HISTORY. CHAPTER TWENTY-TWO BURIED THE omniscient observer—nobody can see everything about everyone. This chapter supplies the second half of that sentence, and the correct mailing address for fear: **there is one party that can see everything about you.**

Then the industry's open secret: the A-book and the B-book. **A-book**: the broker throws your order out into the real market and earns commission and a spread markup—your winning and losing are nothing to it; it earns your "volume." **B-book**: the broker takes your order onto its own book, and **it is your counterparty**—every dollar you lose is a number on the revenue line of its income statement, and your stop order, inside its system, is not a risk warning. **It is an accounts-receivable forecast.** What is most common in reality is the hybrid: your behavioural profile sorts you into a bucket. Clients who lose steadily over the long run stay on the B-book and are held—statistically, money for nothing. The occasional persistent winner is politely A-booked out and handed to the market. This sorting is legal, universal, and **commercially unimpeachable**: EU regulation compels every broker to disclose on its home page what percentage of retail accounts on the platform are losing money—and that number, printed year after year at somewhere around seventy percent, is simultaneously the business plan of the B-book. Taking the other side of a population that statistically loses seven times in ten requires no cheating.

See that layer clearly and several old accounts come to life. The "last look" that Chapter Twenty-Five set aside: certain counterparties, on receiving your order, **take one more look** at the current market—unfavorable to them, rejected; favorable, filled. That is your latency, legally converted into an option they hold. And the anti-obviousness principle of Chapter Twenty-Six has to be applied twice over here: **the party that can see your stop is not only the large money statistically inferring where the cluster sits—it is the firm physically holding your order book.** It does not need to guess where your stop is. It has the list on screen.

The other side of honesty goes down too: this is not a manifesto claiming that brokers are all crooks. Regulated A-book firms, ECN models, the era of negative balance protection are all perfectly real, and plenty of brokers run honest shops. But an incentive structure is a structure and does not shift with good intentions—take inventory of every way this industry earns money: it earns your spread, it earns your volume, it earns your losses. **Not one of the three prospers on your long-run profitability.** At best it is neutral to whether you win or lose. At worst, your losses are its revenue. Your broker can be an honest one. But "we hope you make money" has never appeared in anybody's business plan.

* * *

PUSH THIS CERTAINTY DOWNWARD AND YOU GET THREE COROLLARies.

One: choosing a broker is choosing a counterparty, so run the diligence at counterparty grade. Chapter Seven checked its books (the client money regime); this chapter checks its position. Ask outright which execution model it runs—A-book, B-book, or hybrid—and get the answer in writing. Check what the jurisdiction requires on order execution. Read the mandatory loss-rate disclosure on its own website. This is not one-time homework: models change and owners change—the right to rewrite the rules from Chapter Nine is in force here too.

Two: reduce the surface you expose on its books. The most critical item: **keep your stop logic off its server wherever you can.** This does not conflict with the automation discipline of Chapter Sixteen; it is precisely that discipline in finished form. Write the stop into your own program, running on your own machine, and send the broker a market order only when it triggers—the stop **exists** and **executes automatically** (discipline preserved), but it does not lie on the counterparty's screen as a resting order available for inspection (location kept private). A manual trader cannot reach that level and settles for second best: the anti-obviousness widening of Chapter Twenty-Six, and —do not expose all your capital and all your strategies in one account at one firm (the diversification of Chapter Seven, used a second time, in the dimension of information).

Three: audit your counterparty with data, the way it audits you. It builds a behavioural profile of you; build one of it. Tabulate your slippage distribution every month—**the ratio of positive to negative slippage is the mirror that shows the demon.** Honest execution should be roughly symmetric on both sides; if over the long run you only ever slip the unfavorable way, you are receiving special attention on the B-book. Log the rejection rate, the fill quality in event windows, the speed at which withdrawals land. Find a systematic anomaly and move house. This is the last item on the exemption list of Chapter Seventeen that has not yet drawn its wages: **an institution needs six months of negotiation to change prime brokers. You need a weekend.**

After FXCM was thrown out of the United States, its defenders made an interesting argument: every broker does this, why single us out. That plea may be the single most honest sentence in the entire case. Take the last layer of this chapter away with you: **the first reader of your order is never the market.** Before it reaches any matching engine, it is a letter addressed to your counterparty. You cannot change the postal system. All you get to decide is how much the letter reveals—and who you mail it to.

(End of Chapter Twenty-Seven)

Chapter Twenty-Eight

The Leaking Pool

Certainty 28: After costs, leveraged derivatives trading is a negative-sum game—the pool is certainly negative.

On the question of whether traders actually make money, the human race has conducted exactly one real census.

It was taken in Taiwan. The authorities opened to four finance academics **the complete trading record of the Taiwan Stock Exchange over fifteen years**—1992 to 2006, 3.7 billion transactions, every one of them matched to a specific account. Not a questionnaire, not a sample; no self-reporting, no survivor filter (the full weight of that word is next chapter's business)—a total archive of **every single person who tried, winners and losers, not one missing.** In the history of human trading there is only this one.

The verdict reads as follows. In a typical six-month window, **more than eighty percent of day traders lose money.** Across the fifteen calendar years, day traders as a group were net losers in fourteen. The survival curve: still trading one year after entry, 44%; two years, 24%; three years, **15%**. Those the statistics will certify as predictably and reliably profitable: fewer than **1%**—a few thousand people out of 450,000 day traders. And when the accounts of all individual investors are totaled, the money they lose every year comes to roughly **2.2% of Taiwan's GDP**—very nearly three times what Americans lose in casinos over a full year, measured as a share of GDP. Where did that money go? The data is equally clear: corporations, dealers, foreign investors, funds—**every institutional line is positive.**

But the deepest number in the archive hides in the column for the heaviest traders, and it deserves a line of its own:

The gross profits of heavy day traders are positive. Before costs, the most active people in the entire market took in an average of more than NT$36 million a day between them—their stock selection, their feel for the tape, beat the other side in hard cash. Then subtract costs: an average **net loss** of NT$69 million a day. Commissions and taxes did not merely swallow the whole gross profit, they took the same amount over again. **They beat each other. They lost to the rent.**

* * *

THAT NUMBER DRAGS THIS CHAPTER'S CERTAINTY OFF THE MORAL plane and back to where it was born: arithmetic.

There are two kinds of game in a market. **Positive-sum**: holding equities for the long run without leverage—corporate earnings, dividends, economic growth, water poured into the pool from **outside** without stopping. The cake grows, and every holder can win slowly together; that, in its entirety, is the basis for "time is your friend." **Zero-sum**: derivatives, foreign exchange, CFDs—behind every long contract there necessarily stands a short (the counterparty law of Chapter Twenty-Six), and the two sides' gains and losses mirror each other to the penny. No dividend flowing in, no growth accruing to anyone,

not one source of water outside the pool. The cake is fixed, and every mouthful you take comes out of somebody else's mouth.

Then the rent starts coming out: the spread (the green square of Chapter Four), commission, swap (Chapter Five), slippage (the invoice of Chapter Twenty-Five)—every fill, the pool leaks once. Zero-sum minus rent: **the pool is certainly negative.** How negative is decided by a single multiplication: aggregate turnover × cost per unit. Taiwan's day traders demonstrated that multiplication at its limit—gross positive, net negative; **the skill of the entire population was insufficient to cover the leak rate it generated itself.** This is no Taiwanese peculiarity. India's regulator recently published its own census of the options market: somewhere around nine in ten individual derivatives traders lose money, more than twenty billion dollars lost over three years. Every leveraged pool on earth prints the same verdict.

Once the arithmetic is clear, several old items resolve at a stroke. That "roughly seventy percent of accounts are losing money" printed on every EU broker's home page in Chapter Twenty-Seven—it holds steady year after year not because retail traders happen all to be stupid: **a zero-sum pool that leaks continuously must, arithmetically, manufacture a majority of losers.** Layer on the compounding asymmetry of Chapter Thirteen and the distribution of losers gets stretched further into a long tail—a great many small losers, a very few large winners. The tragedy is not character. First of all it is geometry.

And the question from Chapter Twenty-One loses every last inch of room to dodge inside a negative-sum pool. In a positive-sum market you can still say vaguely, "the money I make is the money of economic growth"—water really is coming in from outside. In a negative-sum pool, **every dollar of profit has a**

specific person funding it: your profit = someone's loss + the rent you have already paid, and the two sides of that equation must balance to the penny. The pool recognizes only four honest sources of income, and they are exactly the rent map of Chapter Twenty-One. **The hedger's premium**—the exporter locking a rate, the airline locking a fuel price; they do not enter the pool to win, they pay rent voluntarily to buy certainty. This is the pool's only positive inflow from outside, and it is the whole of the speculation industry's economic license. **Large money's execution** (Chapter Twenty). **Retail behavior** (those home-made shackles of Chapter Twenty-One). **The forced liquidation of leverage** (Chapter Twelve). Outside those four channels there is no fifth kind of money.

Finally, turn the other face of this certainty upward, so that it does not get read as a letter telling you to quit: **negative-sum is not a death sentence, it is an entry requirement.** That sub-1% of persistent winners is real, and identifiable year by year—the Taiwan data shows that of those once in the top profit group, about two-thirds were still profitable in the following period. The skill is genuine; it is merely extremely scarce. The pool forbids nobody to win. It simply writes the threshold out in plain sight: **your edge has to be real enough to cover your own leak rate, with something left over.** Rowing against the current is not impossible. But measure the current before you talk about the oars.

* * *

PUSH THIS CERTAINTY DOWNWARD AND YOU GET THREE COROLLARIES.

One: split your wealth into two waters and never let them connect. The bulk of your long-term wealth goes into the positive-sum water—unlevered, counted in decades, the source outside the pool doing the work for you. Into the negative-sum pool goes only capital backed by a **verified edge**, treated as the working capital of a business. Two sets of books, two sets of expectations, two states of mind. And one iron rule: **never transfuse from the investment account into the trading account.** That is not topping up a position, that is running a mains pipe into a leaking pool—no supply is generous enough to fill a pool with a hole in it.

Two: in a negative-sum pool, cutting costs is pure alpha. Your personal leak rate = your turnover × your cost per unit. With the same edge, halving costs is worth roughly as much as doubling the edge—and cutting costs requires no forecasting ability at all; it pays out on every trade. Taiwan's heavy traders proved it in hard cash: **what they lacked was not skill. It was accounting.** "Trading less is a direct source of profit" from Chapter Four, and "take off the shackles you made yourself" from Chapter Twenty-One, both compound at double the rate inside a negative-sum pool.

Three: the statement of rent source is upgraded to mandatory in a negative-sum pool. Every strategy answers where the money comes from by picking one of four: the hedger's premium? Large money's execution? Retail behavior? The forced liquidation of leverage? If you can pick one, write it into the statement and re-check periodically that the have-to is still there. **If you cannot pick one, liquidate and leave the pool.** Because in a zero-sum pool that leaks without stopping, for the person who cannot answer "who am I planning to have lose," the answer to that question is himself.

The survival curve in the Taiwan archive is worth one last look: one year, 44%; two years, 24%; three years, 15%. The overwhelming majority of those who left were not beaten on any particular day—**they were ground away by the rent, one notch at a time**, slowly enough that they went on believing the problem lay in their technique. There is no such thing, in a negative-sum pool, as a market where everybody makes money. There never was. There is only you, the person on the other side, and the rent, always being collected. Which makes the last question before you enter not "can I win" but "**who am I planning to have lose**." Anyone who cannot answer it need not wait for the market to reveal the answer.

(End of Chapter Twenty-Eight)

Chapter Twenty-Nine

The Planes That Did Not Come Back

Certainty 29: Every track record you are able to see has already been filtered by death.

1943, New York, Columbia University. In an office with "Statistical Research Group" on the door sat the finest mathematicians wartime America could assemble. The military sent over a set of data and asked them to solve an optimization problem.

The data was **a map of the bullet holes in bombers that came home**. The sample was ample, the pattern clear: holes densely covering the fuselage and the wings, while around the engines and the cockpit the metal was nearly clean. The military's question was a practical one. Armor is heavy, and too much of it eats range and maneuverability, so it can only go where it matters most—and on this data, that means armoring the fuselage and the wings, where the holes cluster. Correct?

One member of the group, a mathematician who had fled Vienna, Abraham Wald, gave the answer that has since been written into every statistics textbook there is: **exactly the opposite—the armor goes where the holes are not.**

Because the data had been collected at the wrong door. It counted the planes that **came back**. A fuselage riddled with holes that still flew home tells you that hits to the fuselage do not kill. And the engines are clean not because flak cannot find an engine, **but because the planes hit in the engine are lying on the floor of the English Channel, and were never eligible for the chart**. A region with few holes is not a safe zone. It is the entrance to the graveyard, and the cleanest part of the map is the label on the deadliest part of the plane. What the military was looking at was not "where do planes get hit," it was "**where can a plane get hit and still come back**"—a few words apart, and the conclusion inverts.

* * *

EIGHTY YEARS ON, THAT MAP IS STILL BEING REDRAWN EVERY DAY. Only the wings have been replaced by equity curves.

Open any fund league table, any signal-seller ranking, any copy-trading platform's page of stars, and every curve you are looking at is **a plane that came back**. The filtering mechanism behind that sample can be said in one line, and both halves of the line are certain: **the leaderboard does not display corpses—the platform has no incentive, and the dead have no ability.** No incentive: the liquidated fund, the blown-up signal, the closed account generate not one new piece of business, so they come down off the page. No ability: the man who lost it all and left does not post, does not update, does not appear in anyone's screenshots—he has taken his bullet holes down to the bottom of the sea. Two forces pointing the same way, and their resultant can only produce one kind of gallery: **a gallery that hangs survivors only.** This is nobody's conspiracy. It is structure—and because it is structure, it never misses.

How large is the distortion? Finance has dissected this one quantitatively. Mutual funds: over a window of fifteen or twenty years, **about half of all funds disappear**—liquidated or merged away—and the overwhelming majority of the disappeared are losers. Strike the corpses from the sample and the category average is systematically inflated; the classic academic estimates run to **one or two percentage points a year**. One set of numbers gets quoted over and over: for a large fund category from 1995 to 2004, the surviving funds averaged 10.8% a year—put the dead funds back in and recompute, and it is **8.9%**. Those two points are the thickness of the gallery's filter. Hedge funds are worse. The databases run on voluntary reporting: when performance rolls over a fund quietly stops reporting, and new funds tend to join only after a strong first year or two, **backfilling those good early years into the record when they do**. Survivorship bias stacked on backfill bias—the studies put the combined inflation at several percentage points a year. As for the retail world, the signal leaderboards and the screenshots on social media, that is the far end of the spectrum: dead accounts evaporate on the spot, the gallery is rehung daily, and the filter is too thick for anyone to measure.

And there is a layer beneath that, one most people never think of: **this law is pointed at you as well.** You tested a hundred strategy ideas and published the one with the prettiest backtest—that curve is a survivor too. It is the one plane in a hundred that came back, and the trust you place in it is built on pretending the other ninety-nine never existed. (Statistics calls this multiple testing. It is survivorship bias in its laboratory form.) One layer deeper still: your memory is itself a gallery—the brilliant trades get replayed, the stupid losses get quietly filed away. Every trader's sense of "how good I am" is a sample with the corpses removed. Chapter Eleven said that any living curve has a maximum historical drawdown that is an underestimate—that is survivorship bias in its time-dimension form: **the reason you can still look at it is that it has not died yet, and "not dead yet" is itself the filter.**

* * *

PUSH THIS CERTAINTY DOWNWARD AND YOU GET THREE COROLLARIES.

One: before reading any track record, find the denominator. What a return curve means depends entirely on the full denominator standing behind it: how many aircraft took off in that formation? A return with no visible denominator gets treated as advertising—not because you suspect it of lying, but because even if it is true, it is only true of the one that came back. Which reorders the weights when you assess a signal source or a fund: **how long it has been alive carries more information than how much it has made.** Returns can be backfilled, can be survivorship, can be luck. Time survived cannot be faked. Look back at that surviving curve in Chapter Twenty-Eight—44% in the first year, 15% over three—and the bare fact of living through three years is the one medal in this industry that is hardest to counterfeit.

Two: fit your own research process with a recorder that keeps every wreck. Every strategy idea you test goes on the register—including, and especially, the ones that died. The true success rate of your methodology is the survivors divided by **all of them**, not the survivors divided by the ones you remember. Before you publish any backtest, declare it to yourself: which attempt number is this? Discount by the number. Then back to the old conclusion of Chapter Eight, which now has a third reason standing behind it: **walk-forward is the only file that cannot be backfilled**—a backtest can be selected out of a hundred attempts, while forward performance can only grow from this moment on, one day at a time, and nobody can run it ahead on your behalf.

Three, the commercial corollary: the full sample is the scarcest honesty in this industry. Since everyone is selling survivors, a record that keeps the dead intact—every signal that failed, every strategy that died, displayed as it was—is by definition a good that nobody is supplying. To anyone who keeps statistics, produces content, or runs any business built on a track record: **everyone else sells survivors, you sell the truth.** That is not a moral posture, it is a moat—because anyone can open a gallery and nobody will build the graveyard, and the genuinely professional buyer trusts only the archive that comes with one. As a consumer, there is exactly one corresponding action: ask any provider of a track record for the list of the dead. The ones who refuse have just been appraised.

History wrote the ending of this story itself, and made it a heavy circle. In 1950 Wald traveled to India to lecture; the plane went down in the mountains, and the man who taught the world how to think about the planes that did not come back did not come back, together with his wife. The map of bullet holes he left behind now hangs above every trader's screen, waiting for you to look up: **when you read any track record, look first for the ones that are not on the chart—they are not on it, and they are the entire meaning of it.** The armor always goes where the holes are not.

(End of Chapter Twenty-Nine)

Finale and Exit

Chapter Thirty

The Thermometer That Heats the Room

Certainty 30: The reflexive loop certainly exists—price is both effect and cause.

In 2017 the US stock market passed through the quietest year in its history.

The VIX, the fear index, posted its lowest annual average on record; the S&P 500 went more than three hundred trading days without a single 2% decline. In that dead-calm water one business swelled into a national sport: **shorting volatility**—betting that the market would stay quiet. The flagship product was called XIV, VIX spelled backwards, a note tracking volatility futures inversely: every point volatility fell, it rose one. In 2017 it more than doubled. Retail poured in, hedge funds put on size; in the first month of 2018 short-volatility products took in another two billion dollars and more, and the market's net short-volatility exposure hit an all-time peak on February 1. The trade was quiet, crowded, and profitable year after year. It was like picking money up off the ground.

Monday, February 5, 2018. The fuse was thoroughly unremarkable: a stronger-than-expected employment and wages report a few days earlier, rate-hike expectations firming, equities pulling back—the S&P fell 4.1% on the day. Not small, but hardly a catastrophe; history is full of meaner days than that. **The catastrophe happened in the fifteen minutes after the four o'clock close.**

The VIX went from 17 to 37 that day, up 115%, the largest single-day percentage spike ever recorded. XIV's prospectus described its engine, and in the same breath its death sentence: to hold its daily inverse-one-times objective, it had to **rebalance at every day's close**—and on a day when volatility exploded, it had to **buy** volatility futures to cut its short exposure. Run the numbers for that evening, and the volatility position XIV and its cousins were obliged to buy into the close comes out, on the various after-the-fact estimates, anywhere from hundreds of millions to billions of dollars—the methodology is still being argued over today, but not one estimate has ever said "zero." So from four o'clock to a quarter past, a machine ran in full view of the market: **buy volatility → volatility gets bought higher → more must be bought → higher still.** VIX futures briefly punched through 50 after hours. XIV's value fell from the previous session's close of 108.37 to **4.22** across those fifteen minutes and the after-hours session that followed—down 96%. Note what those two numbers are: both are indicative values, computed by formula by the calculation agent. During the regular session that day, XIV's closing trade was still printing at $99. The last number holders saw on their screens was more than twenty times the truth. Three days later the note was accelerated and redeemed at $5.99 apiece.

The next day Credit Suisse invoked the sleeping clause on page S-43 of the prospectus—a single-day fall to less than 20% of the prior closing value gives the issuer the right to terminate—and announced the wind-up of XIV. A product that had absorbed billions and printed money for years running was dead in one evening. Traders gave the night a name: **Volmageddon**.

Be clear about the cause of death; it is worth stating in a full sentence. **XIV was not killed by the market—the S&P fell 4%. It was killed by its own hedging: the buying it did to hedge volatility manufactured the volatility that killed it.** The thermometer heated the room, and then melted itself down inside it.

* * *

THE LOOP HAS A NAME. SOROS CALLS IT **REFLEXIVITY**, AND DEFINES the market in a single line: participants act on price, and their actions constitute price—the market is the only kind of system in this world in which **the thermometer itself heats the room**. This is the book's thirtieth certainty, and the last one about the market. It comes in three movements. The first two are the ceiling. The third is where you get to live.

Movement one, the structure is certain: the loop must exist. There is no "true value" sitting in the market independent of its participants, waiting to be discovered—only a consensus that rewrites itself without pause. This is not a matter of philosophical taste; look back and every character in this book has been soaking in the loop the whole time. Why do trends persist? Execution flow manufactures persistence (Chapter Twenty), persistence draws followers, and the followers' buying extends the persistence—a trend runs on two engines, one physical, one a loop. Why is a stop cluster a fuel tank (Chapter Twenty-Six)? Because that is the loop **written into resting orders, in mechanized form**: the fall triggers the selling, the selling deepens the fall. The margin spiral (Chapter Twelve), the collapse of correlations in a crisis (Chapter Fifteen)—and XIV, the loop **turned into a product**: human beings packaged a feedback loop into a note, then pressed the start button with their own hands.

Movement two, the spark cannot be predicted—and that is a theorem, not a regret. The loop amplifies initial differences exponentially, which makes precise long-run prediction impossible in principle: not for want of data, not for want of compute. The mathematics has sealed it shut. The butterfly that starts the storm is not special—it simply happened to beat its wings at the system's critical point, **and it does not know that either**. That employment report was no different in kind from the hundred reports before it; it became the spark not because of its energy but because of the dryness where it landed. And here an equally important correction has to be added: **sensitivity is distributed through the system very unevenly.** The same butterfly can beat its wings all its life in the Himalayas and warm nothing but itself, and in the wet heat of the Amazon can hook itself into the chain that becomes a storm. The same sell order, dropped into a thickly liquid midday, does not raise a ripple; dropped into the vacuum hours, at the mouth of a stop cluster, over the head of a crowded position, it is the grain of sand that brings the critical point down. **All sparks are equal. No two parts of the forest are.**

Movement three: the spark cannot be measured, but the dryness of the forest has a reading. This is the door left open for you underneath the ceiling. The instruments for dryness have in fact already been handed over, one by one, in this book: spread and depth—the market's breathing (Chapter Eighteen); crowding—the concentration of the consensus position

(Chapter Fifteen); and the one most easily read backwards, **how long low volatility has been held down**. Look back at the forest before 2018: the lowest volatility on record, the most crowded short-volatility position on record, a feedback mechanism written out in public in a prospectus. Every line of the dryness index was flashing red, and had been flashing for a year. Calm is not safety; **the longer the calm, the less it is**—because a long quiet tempts everyone to add leverage, to crowd onto the same side, to run the risk models up to the limit of their allowance, and the system's sensitivity to the very same spark gets turned quietly up to maximum with nobody noticing. The most peaceful market is the most dangerous one. That is not old traders' superstition, it is the engineering of reflexivity.

* * *

WITH THAT, THE TRIPLE LOCK ON THE MARKET'S UNPREDICTABILITY is fully fitted: **the orders that exist right now, you cannot see all of** (Chapter Twenty-Two, the window problem); **the intentions of the future do not exist** (Chapter Twenty-Three, the existence problem); **and even if the intentions did exist, they would be rewritten continuously by everybody's collective behavior** (this chapter, the loop problem). Three locks, each engaging the next, welding the project of "solving the market" shut inside the impossible.

But notice what the three locks have not locked. What they seal is **prediction**, not **survival**, and certainly not profit—the road this book has walked out again and again is still wide open beneath all three: **do not predict the spark, measure the dryness, then ride somebody else's have-to.** Nobody needed to predict February 5 to get through the XIV night: the people reading dryness had cut size and cut leverage long before. And that volatility position that had to be bought that evening—whose have-to was that? A have-to written into a prospectus, executed mechanically, on public view to the whole market. Every single person standing on the other side of it was collecting rent.

One last layer, and the mirror turns to face you: **your strategy is a participant in the loop too.** An edge used by enough people changes the market it trades and blunts itself—half of backtest decay is overfitting, and the other half is reflexivity eating you. This gives forward validation its third and deepest justification: it is not only testing whether the edge is real (Chapter Eight) and whether it is a survivor (Chapter Twenty-Nine), it is **listening continuously for whether the crowd has worn the edge away**. From which comes the last design discipline in this book: leave your rules a little personality—do not round your parameters, do not place where everyone places, do not chase the signal everyone is buying—**in a market made of loops, being identical to everybody else is itself a risk.**

* * *

PUSH THIS CERTAINTY DOWNWARD AND YOU GET THREE COROLlaries—and the gathering-in of the whole book's method.

One: build dryness into a dashboard. Three readings: how long volatility has been suppressed, spread and depth, and the overlap between your positions and the market consensus. When the index is high—cut leverage, widen stops, check whether you are standing on the crowded side. You do not have to predict the spark; the spark cannot be predicted. The state of the forest can be checked any day of the week.

Two: audit what your own rules look like when they are executed collectively. Everyone's stop in the same place makes a cluster; everyone's signal from the same bestseller makes a crowd. Take every rule you own and imagine a million people executing it at the same moment—does it turn on you? If it does, give it a shift that belongs to you alone. **In a market of loops, personality is not a style. It is a fortification.**

Three: add the last column to the statement of rent source. The declaration of Chapter Twenty-One gets one more line: "Could this have-to be dissolved by too many people collecting rent on it?" Structural constraints—execution always leaves a trace, settlement runs on a calendar—are close to perpetual; behavioral constraints, the habits of retail, migrate; and **crowded alpha kills itself**—those money-printing XIV returns were precisely the summons that carried it to the graveyard. Your forward data is the only stethoscope for any of it.

Coda. A few years after XIV died, short-volatility products came back to market under new names with the leverage dialed down, and gathered a new generation of rent collectors around them—the loop does not die, because the participants are always human. The first twenty-nine certainties described every part of this machine; the thirtieth explains why the machine as a whole **can never be completely solved**: it changes when it is observed, it bites back when it is exploited, and when it is predicted it rewrites the prediction. This is not a defect in the market. **This is the definition of a market.**

Fortunately, you never needed to solve it. And this machine that never stops turning has left you one last gift—the one thing on the whole food chain that only you possess. Last chapter. Open the door and collect it.

(End of Chapter Thirty · The Finale)

Chapter Thirty-One

The Door

Certainty 31: Staying flat is always a legal option—the one certain structural advantage belonging to the bottom of the food chain.

For the last chapter, call the whole cast out one more time. This time everyone gets the same single question:

"Are you free not to trade?"

The Virtus of this world, the market maker with 1,237 winning days—no. Continuous two-sided quoting is its charter, its license, its mode of existence; a market maker that stops quoting is not resting, it is dying. The fund manager—no. His mandate requires him to hold, the benchmark humiliates his cash balance every day, and the redemption terms let clients force his chips out of him at the bottom of any hole; sit flat for three months? That is called operating outside mandate, and it is the standard wording in a termination letter. Sovereigns and central banks—no; a policy mission takes no holidays. The whale—no; a hundred-billion position is its very existence, and to exit is to trigger the landslide. The exporter with a hedge on—no; the risk grows inside his business, and not hedging is running naked. The broker—no; no matching, no revenue. Even that tax partner who never loses is chained by law to his post at the tollbooth.

Ask the entire food chain and every tier is wearing irons—which is exactly the rent map drawn in Chapter Twenty-One: **every shackle is somebody's income.**

And then it is the turn of the lowest seat on the chain, the least conspicuous one. You.

You are free. Indefinitely. At zero cost. Do not trade today, and no benchmark humiliates you; do not trade this month, and no client redeems; do not trade this year, and no board calls you to account. The moment you close the laptop, there is not one document, not one charter, not one person in this entire market with the authority to order you back.

Thirty chapters have inventoried every certainty in this market, and every one of them is somebody's shackle. Only at the last square do you discover that one thing exists on this chain and exists nowhere else along it: **a seat that carries no structural have-to of any kind.** And it has been yours the whole time.

* * *

THIS IS NOT A CONSOLATION PRIZE. USE THE BOOK'S OWN theorems and put a price on the door.

Chapter Twenty-Eight proved the pool is certainly negative: the average action of all participants has an expectation below zero. Which means that staying flat—the one action whose expectation is exactly zero—**mathematically beats the average participant in the pool outright**. Doing nothing beats most of the people on the floor: that is not inspirational syrup, it is the subtraction on a leaking pool. Chapter Fourteen said all market liquidity is procyclical and the only countercyclical liquidity is the kind you brought yourself—the man who is not forced, on the day everyone else is forced, is the only buyer in the building, and the have-to he collects on is the fattest one there is. Chapter Thirty taught you to measure the dryness of the forest —and when every gauge is red, the institutions have to stay in the woods. **You can leave for the whole season.** Chapter Twenty-Four said the image needs exposure to develop—and while the image is blurred you can decline the bet and wait for it to sharpen; on the entire chain, only you enjoy the luxury of taking only the few shots where the image has developed clearly. The freeze line of Chapter Eleven and the intervention rules of Chapter Sixteen are executable at all on one condition and one only: **you own the right to stop.** Chapter Ten said position size is the only variable under your one-hundred-percent control—and flat is that variable's zero point: always reachable, always legal, always free.

One door, and it is simultaneously excess return, countercyclical liquidity, a refuge, an option and a brake. Every weapon this book has written about has a grip that runs back to it.

So where is the tragedy? Chapter Twenty-One already made the diagnosis: **retail is the only species on the whole food chain that invents its own have-tos.** Have to watch the screen every day. Have to win back yesterday's loss. Have to be fully loaded or the capital is going to waste. Bored, and so have to find a trade. Not one of them is written in any document; every one was welded on by the man wearing it. And every weld seals the door a little further shut. The way the overwhelming majority of people lose everything is not that they were outclassed—**it is that they voluntarily surrendered the only exemption on the entire chain, and then went out to fight a battle without institutional resources while wearing the institutions' irons.**

And see this clearly: it is not all your own weakness. It is a whole industry in conspiracy. The broker wants your volume (Chapter Twenty-Seven), the signal seller wants your subscription, financial content wants your anxiety, and the "here comes the opportunity" push notification is touting customers for the green square (Chapter Four)—**every minute you spend using that door, the entire food chain collects nothing.** So the industry holds one tacit common interest: to make you forget the door is there. They package patience as a virtue—because a virtue can be praised, and then ignored. **Nobody tells you it is a weapon. Because weapons get used.**

* * *

PUSH THIS CERTAINTY DOWNWARD AND YOU GET THREE COROLlaries—the last three in the book.

One: write "do not trade" into the system as a formal position state. Flat should not be the blank space left over when no opportunity was found. Like an entry, it should have trigger conditions of its own: the dryness gauge red (Chapter Thirty), the image not developed (Chapter Twenty-Four), an event window (Chapter Eighteen), drawdown touching the line (Chapter Eleven)—any one of them hits and the system outputs FLAT, with exactly the solemnity with which it outputs BUY. Then measure the share of your time spent flat: **a man whose share is too low is not industrious, he is paying behavioral rent.** Promote "not doing it" from a character flaw to a system instruction.

Two: rehearse closing the door on a schedule. Once a quarter, set a mandatory period out of the market—a few days is enough—and verify you can still get a grip on the handle. For the man who cannot, the door is already welded shut, and the thirty chapters before this were wasted on him. Use the time away for real work: run the system review of Chapter Eleven, read the forward log of Chapter Eight, go through the rent declaration of Chapter Twenty-One line by line. **The market seen from behind the door and the market seen from the floor are two different markets. Go out through it at least a few times a year.**

Three: remember that the door swings both ways, but the hinge has to be a rule. You may decline to enter, and you may decline to stay: the lease expires (the constraint is released, the death monitor on the Chapter Twenty-One declaration goes off), the freeze line trips, the dryness gauge pegs—**when the rule says go, go.** But the door is never driven by emotion. Bolting for the exit in a panic is not using the door, it is getting caught in it. The door is part of the discipline, not an excuse for escape—and that distinction is the final appearance of the line from Chapter Sixteen: all of your free will is exercised in the legislature, none of it during execution.

* * *

NOW THE LEDGER CAN BE CLOSED.

Thirty certainties—from the accident written on the timetable to two promises of which only one is kept; from the green square to five o'clock on Wednesday; from money on someone else's books to the eight hours that never happened; from a coin that keeps its word to the twenty-sixth black; from the waterline, the window and the starlight to where the inventory comes from and the first reader; from the leaking pool and the planes that did not come back to that thermometer which heated the room—**thirty of them, and every one is a wall.** Together they fence in the true shape of this market: on your cost side every item is certain, on your return side nothing is promised at all; every have-to you carry is being rented out by somebody, and the only rent you can ever collect is on somebody else's have-to.

The title of this book can now be written out in full: **the only certainties in trading are your costs and other people's have-tos—and your own don't-have-to.** Your costs are the rent you are certain to pay; other people's have-tos are your only source of rent; and the don't-have-to is the one thing in the building that neither pays rent nor collects it —

A door.

The top of the food chain has never been the smartest, or the fastest, or the richest—**it is the one wearing the fewest shackles.** And you, the smallest participant in this market, happen to have been born in the seat nearest the door. If only one thing can be carried out of these thirty-one chapters, let it not be any piece of knowledge but a kind of eyesight: **the eyesight that sees shackles**—see other people's, and collect the rent; see your own, and cut them off.

You have seen the walls. The door has been open all along.

(End of Chapter Thirty-One · End of Book)

The Thirty-Second

This book has inventoried thirty-one certainties. Before it closes, one last one is owed to you:

The Thirty-Second: this book certainly contains errors and omissions—and part of it will expire as enough people read it.

The first half is the honesty of Chapter Twenty-Nine. These thirty-one were filtered by the author out of a larger field of candidates; the ones abandoned, you cannot see. The author, too, is a plane that came back. So use the filter this book taught you on the book itself: find its denominator, check its grammar, ask of every proposition where the money comes from. Only if it holds up does it deserve to be used by you.

The second half is the verdict of Chapter Thirty. If enough people move their stops the way Chapter Twenty-Six says, the clusters will migrate. If enough people hold behind the door the way Chapter Thirty-One says, the rent structure of the pool will change. The market this book describes will be altered by the people who have read this book—**it, too, is a participant in the loop.** The entries in here that are close to physics—the counterparty, latency, the arithmetic of compounding—will not budge; the ones growing on the behavior of crowds have a shelf life the crowd decides. Which belongs to which, the book has already given you the test for. The judgment, from here, is yours.

So the correct use of this book was never to memorize thirty-one conclusions. It is to walk out with the ruler—the ruler that measures only whether a thing is certain, and never whether it sounds good. Take it to your market, your system, your next ten years. Find the thirty-second, and the thirty-third. Or overturn one of the ones in here.

On the day you actually do it, you stop being this book's reader.

You are its peer. Send the author yours; it will be welcome.

(The End)

Notes and References

Sources for the real events, institutions, figures, and research discussed in this book are listed below. Where an original document exists—from a regulator, exchange, central bank, court, or academic publication—it is cited as the primary source; where only media reporting is available, that is noted in the entry.

Chapter 1 · The Accident Written on the Timetable

· The yen flash crash of 3 January 2019: post-mortem analysis by the Reserve Bank of Australia (*The Recent Japanese Yen Flash Event*, Statement on Monetary Policy, February 2019). rba.gov.au/publications/smp/2019/feb/box-b-the-recent-japanese-yen-flash-event.html

· Negative-balance losses at Japanese STP brokers: industry tally by Finance Magnates, totaling roughly ¥943 million. financemagnates.com

· The sterling flash crash of 7 October 2016: official report by the BIS Markets Committee, *The sterling "flash event" of 7 October 2016*. bis.org/publ/mktc09.htm

Chapter 2 · Two Promises, One Kept

· The Swiss National Bank's abandonment of the 1.20 EUR/CHF floor (15 January 2015): SNB official statements and subsequent commentary. snb.ch

· Client negative balances and a debt of £21,171: the client was Jan Nowak; FX Markets, *IG under fire from clients with huge negative balances* (19 March 2015). Some 350 IG clients were affected and 327 went to negative balances, for about £18.5 million in total.

· The matter never reached court: clients complained to the FCA and brought a group complaint to the Financial Ombudsman Service, which found the fills could have been better; IG repriced and absorbed roughly £1 million (Bloomberg, 7 October 2015).

- Alpari UK's insolvency: Reuters reporting (January 2015).
- FXCM's roughly $225 million in client negative-balance losses: company disclosure.
- Second-by-second execution and liquidity data: FXCM, *FXCM Releases Detailed Data on the SNB Flash Crash* (press release, 12 March 2015).

Chapter 3 · A Straight Line, Three Milliseconds Long

- The Spread Networks line: built at a cost of roughly $300 million by about 2,000 workers over 827 miles, cutting round-trip latency to roughly 13 milliseconds.
- Sold to Zayo for $127 million in 2017: Zayo press release. zayo.com/newsroom
- The claim that "Wall Street extracts roughly $20 billion a year from the price gap between the two markets": the builder's own estimate, not an independently audited figure.

Chapter 5 · Five O'Clock on Wednesday

- Herstatt Bank's license was revoked on Wednesday, 26 June 1974: losses of DM 470 million against capital of DM 44 million. Historical accounts give three different times for the revocation—14:40, 15:30, and 16:30.
- The Basel Committee on Banking Supervision was established at the end of 1974 in response to the episode: BIS official history. bis.org/bcbs/history.htm
- CLS (Continuous Linked Settlement) went live on 9 September 2002: Deutsche Bundesbank. bundesbank.de
- Herstatt risk and FX settlement: BIS Quarterly Review, *FX settlement risk* (December 2002).

Chapter 6 · The Partner Who Never Loses

- Bitcoin's all-time high of more than $68,000 on 8 November 2021: CNBC.
- The $3,000-per-year cap on capital-loss deductions under US tax law: IRS rules.

Chapter 7 · Money on Someone Else's Books

- MF Global's bankruptcy on 31 October 2011, the eighth-largest bankruptcy in US history, with a customer-fund shortfall of roughly $1.6 billion: Congressional Research Service report R42091, *The MF Global Bankruptcy, Missing Customer Funds, and Proposals for Reform.*
- Full return of customer funds: SIPC press release, April 2014. sipc.org
- Tightened restrictions on the investment of segregated customer funds: CFTC Regulation 1.25 final rule (December 2011).

Chapter 8 · The Evening Eraser

- The full sequence of the 6 May 2010 Flash Crash—trades executed at one cent, trades executed at nearly $100,000, and the bulk cancellation of more than 20,000 trades priced more than 60% away from reference: joint SEC-CFTC report, *Findings Regarding the Market Events of May 6, 2010.* sec.gov/files/marketevents-report.pdf
- Accenture's 52-week low showing $17.74 for an extended period: publicly confirmed by then-CFO Pamela Craig.
- Sotheby's traded at $100,000 a share (the official high for the day was later restored to $64.00). The joint report speaks only of prices "as low as one cent or as high as $100,000" and names no individual stock; the widely repeated claim that Apple and Hewlett-Packard also printed near $100,000 traces to a single news blog post that day, with no exchange or regulatory record behind it, and is not relied on here.
- Nasdaq alone broke 10,468 trades—1.41 million shares in 236 securities—between 2:40 and 3:00 p.m.: testimony of Eric Noll, Executive Vice President, NASDAQ OMX, before Congress in May 2010. (The SEC/CFTC preliminary report, on a different basis, counts 20,761 broken trades market-wide, 12,306 of them attributed to Nasdaq.)

Chapter 9 · The Eight Hours That Never Happened

- LME nickel touching $101,365 per tonne at 06:08 on 8 March 2022, trading suspended at 08:15, and the day's trades canceled: judgment of the England and Wales Court of Appeal, *R (Elliott Associates) v London Metal Exchange.*

- The exchange's reliance on Rule 22 of its rulebook was upheld by the court: same judgment.
- The UK Financial Conduct Authority's fine of roughly £9.2 million against the LME in 2025: FCA final notice.
- Comex Silver Rule 7 of 7 January 1980, the liquidation-only order of 21 January, Silver Thursday on 27 March, and silver's peak of $49.45 on 18 January: contemporary reporting and financial histories.
- Exchange governors holding silver shorts: *Fortune*, 28 July 1980, reported that nine of the twenty-three members of the Comex board—dealers and traders, personally and through the firms they represented—held net short positions totaling some 75 million ounces, on data drawn from confidential CFTC position reports and made public by Senator William Proxmire in hearings. The SEC staff report *The Silver Crisis of 1980* (1982) records the same, and also records that the CFTC's subsequent investigation found no provable conflict of interest on the part of any board member.

Chapter 10 · A Coin That Keeps Its Word

- The experiment with 61 participants, $25 in starting capital, and a coin biased 60% toward heads; 28% went bust, 18 bet everything at least once, 7,253 total flips across the room, a 59.6% heads rate, and an average payout of $91: Victor Haghani & Richard Dewey, *Rational Decision-Making Under Uncertainty: Observed Betting Patterns on a Biased Coin* (2016). arXiv: 1701.01427
- Haghani was a founding partner of Long-Term Capital Management.

Chapter 12 · Fifty Bankers

- Tsingshan's short position at roughly five times LME nickel inventory, nickel's rise from about $29,100 to above $100,000 in three days, the LME's suspension of trading through 16 March, and the JPMorgan-led standstill agreement: US Treasury Office of Financial Research working paper OFR WP 24-09, *Central Clearing and Trade Cancellation.*
- More than fifty bankers converging on the office, "we are confident we can get through this," and an eventual close-out loss of roughly $1 billion: reporting by the *South China Morning Post.*

- The ten-billion-dollar figure for paper losses: a contemporary market and media estimate (an $8 billion figure also circulated), not an audited number from any institution.

Chapter 13 · The Shake Tax

- FAS and FAZ launched on the same day, 6 November 2008, both 3x leveraged products on the S&P Financial Select Sector index: Direxion product materials.
- Official performance from inception to the end of 2011: FAS −47.54% annualized, FAZ −75.13% annualized, against +9.48% annualized for the Russell 1000 Financial Services index—cumulative declines of roughly 87% and 99% respectively (roughly 85% and 99% measured to autumn 2011): Direxion summary prospectuses filed with the SEC (Form 497K, 28 February 2012).
- Both declines were masked by reverse splits: by autumn 2011 FAZ had contracted 50:1 cumulatively.
- Volatility drag in leveraged and inverse ETFs: Minder Cheng & Ananth Madhavan, *The Dynamics of Leveraged and Inverse Exchange-Traded Funds* (2009); SLCG, *Leveraged ETFs, Holding Periods and Investment Shortfalls* (measured November 2008–June 2010: underlying up 10%, FAS −72.4%, FAZ −97.9%).

Chapter 14 · The Deepest Ocean

- The 64-basis-point rise in ten-year Treasury yields between 9 and 18 March 2020, with selling pressure from mutual funds and foreign official institutions: BIS Working Paper 966, *The Treasury market in spring 2020 and the response of the Federal Reserve.*
- The $1.5 trillion repo operation on 12 March: New York Fed operational announcement. newyorkfed.org
- The shift to open-ended, "in the amounts needed" bond purchases on 23 March: Federal Reserve press release.
- Treasury purchases of roughly $72 billion a day: the New York Fed's 23 March statement set a pace of "approximately $75 billion of Treasury securities ... each business day"; the Fed's own H.4.1 release shows Treasury holdings rising $362.5 billion in the week to 1 April, or about $72.5 billion

per business day. This is the late-March peak, measured per business day rather than per calendar day.

Chapter 15 · The Only Thing That Rose That Day

- The model's projected worst case of $35 million versus an actual loss of $553 million on 21 August 1998: Roger Lowenstein, *When Genius Failed: The Rise and Fall of Long-Term Capital Management* (2000).
- The 44% loss in August alone, two Nobel laureates in economics among the partners, and the $3.6 billion recapitalization by fourteen banks on 23 September in exchange for a 90% stake: Federal Reserve History, *Near Failure of Long-Term Capital Management*.
- The $1.25 trillion notional figure: testimony of CFTC Chair Brooksley Born, describing the derivatives notional reported at the time of the September 1998 rescue, mostly OTC swaps with the remainder exchange-traded futures. The President's Working Group report of 1999 gives an end-August 1998 breakdown instead—futures above $500 billion, swaps above $750 billion, options and other OTC above $150 billion, some $1.4 trillion in all. The two figures differ in date and in what they include.
- The "ten standard deviations / 3.3×10^{20} years" figure: a widely circulated after-the-fact calculation (see Niall Ferguson, *The Ascent of Money*, 2008, p. 329), not an original output of LTCM's risk model.

Chapter 16 · The Plane No One Man Can Fly

- The crash of the Boeing Model 299 on 30 October 1935, caused by an unreleased gust lock, killing Major Hill and test pilot Tower: National Museum of the US Air Force records. nationalmuseum.af.mil
- After the checklist system was established, the first twelve aircraft of the type flew 1.8 million miles without incident; total B-17 production reached roughly 12,730 aircraft.
- Hill Air Force Base in Utah is named for Major Ployer P. Hill.

Chapter 17 · One Thousand Two Hundred Thirty-Seven Wins, One Loss

- Only one losing day across 1,238 trading days (1 January 2009 to 31 December 2013): Virtu Financial Form S-1, March 2014, SEC EDGAR.

- Only one losing day across 1,485 trading days (1 January 2008 to 20 February 2015): Virtu Financial Form S-1/A, 2015.

Chapter 18 · The Syllabus of Fear

- The Singapore Exchange's margin increase on 17 June 2016, and private notice to dealers from Hong Kong Exchanges and LCH.Clearnet: Reuters reporting.
- Sterling hit a thirty-one-year low on referendum night.
- The sterling flash crash of 7 October 2016: BIS Markets Committee report. On Thomson Reuters Matching execution data, sterling touched 1.1491 at 00:07:41 BST, almost 9% below the pre-event level of 1.26, with the fall beginning at 00:07:03—the deepest part of the move took about forty seconds. The 6% widely quoted in the press corresponds to the Bloomberg composite feed, which bottomed near 1.1841.

Chapter 19 · Don't Mistake Yourself for the Moon

- Japan's yen-buying intervention on 22 September 2022, its first since 1998; ¥6.34 trillion in October; ¥9.18 trillion (roughly $60 billion) combined across September and October: official data from Japan's Ministry of Finance. mof.go.jp

Chapter 20 · The Waterline

- The CDX IG9 index and its constituent spreads, and the growth of JPMorgan's Chief Investment Office position from $51 billion at the end of 2011 to $157 billion by the end of March 2012: US Senate Permanent Subcommittee on Investigations report, *JPMorgan Chase Whale Trades: A Case History of Derivatives Risks and Abuses* (2013).
- Dimon's "tempest in a teapot" remark (13 April 2012), the disclosure of roughly $2 billion in losses on 10 May, and his congressional testimony "I was dead wrong" on 13 June; JPMorgan still posted record net income of $21.3 billion that year: company filings and contemporary reporting.

Chapter 22 · One Window Each

- The New York Attorney General's 2014 suit against Barclays over its dark pool, settled in 2016: a $70 million fine for Barclays, and $60 million in fines plus $24.3 million in restitution for Credit Suisse, totaling $154.3 million: official press release from the Office of the New York Attorney General. ag.ny.gov

- The share of volume executed away from public order books: the SEC's Order Competition Rule proposal tallies first-quarter 2022 US NMS stock volume as 59.7% on exchanges, 10.2% in dark pools, 23.9% internalized by large wholesalers and 6.3% at other brokers—roughly forty percent off-exchange in all. (Cboe puts the off-exchange share at 50.6% in 2025, the first year above half.)

Chapter 23 · Information That Does Not Exist Yet

- Consensus forecasts calling for gains in every one of twenty-five years (2000–2024), seven of which actually closed down; an average absolute miss of 14.2 percentage points; a forecast of +3.9% for 2022 against an actual decline of 19.4% on a price-return basis, a 23.3-point miss and the largest in the series; a forecast of +9.2% for 2008 against an actual decline of 38.5%: the retrospective tally of strategists' annual forecasts compiled by Paul Hickey of Bespoke Investment Group.
- An overall directional accuracy of roughly 47.4% among well-known market pundits: CXO Advisory Group's long-run tracking of sixty-eight "experts."

Chapter 25 · Starlight

- Microwave networks cutting Chicago–New Jersey round-trip latency to roughly 8.2–8.5 milliseconds, approaching the theoretical limit of about 7.9 milliseconds.
- Optimal relay points for cross-market arbitrage often falling in the ocean: A. D. Wissner-Gross & C. E. Freer, *Relativistic Statistical Arbitrage*, Physical Review E 82, 056104 (2010).

Chapter 26 · Where the Inventory Comes From

- The UK FCA's combined fine of £1.115 billion (roughly $1.7 billion) against five banks on 12 November 2014, finding that traders shared confidential client information and attempted to manipulate G10 spot FX fixes and trigger client stop orders; chat-room names included "the players," "the 3 musketeers," and "1 team, 1 dream": FCA final notice. fca.org.uk

- Citigroup, JPMorgan, Barclays, and RBS pleading guilty to criminal charges on 20 May 2015, with fines exceeding $2.5 billion; the "The Cartel" chat room features in the case record: US Department of Justice press release. justice.gov

Chapter 27 · First Reader

- CFTC order of 6 February 2017: FXCM fined $7 million and permanently barred from registering in the US; the order found that a market maker FXCM had incubated took the other side of client trades and kicked back roughly 70% of its monthly trading profits to FXCM, totaling about $77 million from 2010 to 2014: CFTC Press Release 7528-17. cftc.gov
- The same day, the National Futures Association expelled FXCM and three of its principals from membership.

Chapter 28 · The Leaking Pool

- Complete Taiwan Stock Exchange account-level data from 1992 to 2006, showing persistent losses among day traders as a group and fewer than 1% earning consistent profits net of costs: Brad M. Barber, Yi-Tsung Lee, Yu-Jane Liu & Terrance Odean, *The Cross-Section of Speculator Skill: Evidence from Day Trading*, Journal of Financial Markets (2014); and, by the same authors, *Do Day Traders Rationally Learn About Their Ability?*
- Annual trading losses by individual investors amounting to roughly 2.2% of Taiwan's GDP: Barber, Lee, Liu & Odean, *Just How Much Do Individual Investors Lose by Trading?*, Review of Financial Studies.
- 93% of individual traders in India losing money in equity derivatives across FY22–FY24, for combined losses of roughly 1.8 trillion rupees: SEBI press release 37/2024. sebi.gov.in

Chapter 29 · The Planes That Did Not Come Back

- Abraham Wald's classified memorandum for Columbia University's Statistical Research Group, arguing for armor where bullet holes were sparse: *A Method of Estimating Plane Vulnerability Based on Damage of Survivors*, declassified reprint by the Center for Naval Analyses. cna.org
- Abraham Wald and his wife died in a plane crash in the Nilgiri Hills of southern India on 13 December 1950.

- A fund category showing 10.8% annualized for surviving funds over 1995–2004 against 8.9% once the dead funds are put back: from the survivorship measurements across forty-two Morningstar categories in Barrett & Brodeski, *Survivor Bias and Improper Measurement* (2006)—both the window and the 1.9-point gap match that study. Comparable results: CRSP data at the University of Chicago put surviving funds at 11% annualized over forty years against 9.4% including the dead; Malkiel (1995) measured 17.09% against 15.69% for US equity funds over 1982–1991.
- Survivorship bias and backfill bias in hedge fund databases: *Measurement Biases in Hedge Fund Performance Data: An Update*, Financial Analysts Journal (2009).

Chapter 30 · The Thermometer That Heats the Room

- The VIX's rise from 17.31 to 37.32 on 5 February 2018, a one-day gain of 115.6% and the largest single-day percentage move on record; forced rebalancing and reflexive feedback in short-volatility products: Cboe, *After the Volpocalypse*; BIS Quarterly Review (March 2018).
- XIV's indicative value closing at $108.3681 on 2 February; its intraday indicative value falling below 20% of the prior close on 5 February, triggering the accelerated redemption clause; final cash settlement at $5.99 per share: Credit Suisse accelerated redemption notice, SEC EDGAR.
- The dispute over the indicative value around 5:09 p.m. that evening: *Set Capital LLC et al. v. Credit Suisse Group AG*, S.D.N.Y. 1:18-cv-02268, class action complaint.

On What Is Not Cited Here

Some statements in this book are general mathematical facts (the house edge of European roulette at $1/37 \approx 2.703\%$, the arithmetic of recovering from compounding losses, margin formulas) or illustrative examples the author constructed for teaching purposes, and are not separately cited. A few other widely circulated anecdotes lack a primary-source archive (such as the twenty-six consecutive blacks at the Monte Carlo casino in 1913); these appear in the book as illustrations, and readers should weigh them through the filter described in Chapter 29.

www.ingramcontent.com/pod-product-compliance
Lightning Source LLC
LaVergne TN
LVHW010721061126
851857LV00014B/1289